# The Rainbow Serpent

Marie-Louise von Franz, Honorary Patron

**Studies in Jungian Psychology
by Jungian Analysts**

**Daryl Sharp, General Editor**

# The Rainbow Serpent

## Bridge to Consciousness

**ROBERT L. GARDNER**

To Dorothy, Selena and Mandy

**Canadian Cataloguing in Publication Data**

Gardner, Robert L. (Robert Lindsay), 1945-
   The rainbow serpent

(Studies in Jungian psychology by Jungian analysts; 45)

Includes bibliographical references.

ISBN 0-919123-46-5

1. Rainbow serpent—Psychological aspects.
2. Archetype (Psychology). 3. Mythology—Therapeutic use.
4. Jung, C.G. (Carl Gustav), 1875-1961.
I. Title.   II. Series.

BF175.G37 1990     154     C90-094680-6



INNER CITY BOOKS
Box 1271, Station Q, Toronto, Canada M4T 2P4
Telephone (416) 927-0355

Honorary Patron: Marie-Louise von Franz.
Publisher and General Editor: Daryl Sharp.
Senior Editor: Victoria Cowan.

INNER CITY BOOKS was founded in 1980 to promote the
understanding and practical application of the work of C.G. Jung.

*Cover:* Snake of the Marinbata people of Arnhem Land, painting
on hardboard. (Photo by Axel Poignant)

Index by Daryl Sharp.

Printed and bound in Canada by Webcom Limited

# Contents



*See final page for descriptions of other Inner City Books*

Rock painting of the Walbiri tribe of Aborigines
representing the Rainbow Serpent.
(From Francis Huxley, *The Way of the Sacred*)

# Introduction

It is somewhat of a paradox that a country known for the wonders of its natural environment has the most urbanized population of all the continents. With some seventy percent of Australians clustered in the large cities and almost ninety per cent in urban areas,[1] the fabled outback is far from being part of the average Australian's immediate experience.

Growing up in Melbourne, I was one of the seventy per cent, but consider myself privileged because of the amount of time I was able to spend in the outback. Most of these visits were to the Darling River which flows through the semi-arid desert of western New South Wales where I experienced not only some of the brutal power of this severe environment but also its spectacular natural beauty. In this part of Australia the white man has the opportunity to apply a full range of skills in the art of bush-craft. Anyone who has been there can only marvel at the inventiveness it has inspired.

But the real magic was passed on to me through my contacts with the people of the Wuradjeri tribe and the experience of the mysteries of animal and plant life in this seemingly harsh and barren landscape. Though my time there was relatively fleeting, it stirred profound and lasting feelings concerning the difference between the spirit of the land and the culture imposed on it.

This unique contact with the natural and human spirit of the country was to become the source of many dreams I had of aboriginal motifs. It has given a dimension to my life that would not have been there had I stayed behind city walls.

The Australian saying, "Sydney or the bush," succinctly describes the division in the country because it assumes that the choice for an Australian is one or the other, the culture of Sydney or the natural environment. The saying is popularly used as a gambling idiom

---

[1] *Australian Year Book,* 1987, pp. 257-258.

when someone bets everything to become either a big winner or a big loser; Sydney or the bush, wealth or poverty. Such are the respective values placed on the two environments. As long as culture and nature are perceived to be so divergent, there will be an intrinsic disharmony in the country and the nation will be split.

The division is reflected in the historical disregard of the people closest to the land and their exclusion from mainstream Australian life. It is also reflected in the fact that not until 1967 were Aborigines given the legal status of any other Australian, when the Commonwealth assumed the power to enact legislation to abolish constitutional discrimination against them.[2] Until then Aborigines had been largely excluded from the political agenda. This changed in the early 1970s, mainly as a result of debates over land rights. But the struggle over the right to own land is not only a clash of cultures; more particularly it is about two different attitudes toward land itself, which on a personal level symbolizes the feminine nature of man and on a collective level the world soul or *anima mundi.*

Native Australians see the land as an essential part of their religious heritage. The dominant white culture views it as a rich resource to be exploited. The Land Rights Act of 1976 gave Aborigines primary responsibility for particular pieces of land as well as the chance to reclaim sacred sites that had previously been lost to mining and pastoral leases. But, while these and other important advances have been made in opening communications between the two cultures, there is still a sense that they are essentially exclusive of one another.

This book investigates the notion that at a deeper psychological level the two cultures are related and share something more than the fact that they happen to be on the same continent. Jung hypothesized that all humanity shares a common heritage through the collective unconscious, and suggested that the evidence for its existence is seen primarily in spontaneous symbolic expressions.[3] By approaching the

---

[2] See R. Ward, *Australia Since the Coming of Man,* p. 214.

[3] See "Approaching the Unconscious," in C.G. Jung, ed., *Man and His Symbols,* pp. 20ff.

Australian situation from this point of view, the meaning that lies hidden behind such motifs can be investigated, perhaps helping black and white cultures to realize that they share a common language and background.

The myth of the Wawilak women is used to investigate this common ground because it not only describes a process by which the psyche is created but also leads us into a better understanding of the white and black mentalities in Australia. It seems that one is a mirror version of the other. What is accepted by one is rejected by the other. Thus, the myth describes the basis for a neurotic split in which each community represents the unknown or shadow side that is repressed by the other.

Also investigated is the initiation of a Wuradjeri medicine-man as an impressive example of how the opposing psychological principles of the black and white cultures are integrated by one person. In this regard his initiation represents a process of individuation.

Despite my fascination with this abstruse myth I was initially unsure of how to approach it. In the midst of this dilemma my unconscious responded with a helpful dream.

> I am standing next to a tall, regal aboriginal man. We are looking out into the vast outback toward the horizon. Closer to us are some aboriginal and white women walking around on the rich red earth.

The dream suggests that, in general terms, the black and white views of the country should be the focus of this work. The man with whom I am standing is clearly a very impressive figure who commands respect and special attention. Since he is taller than I and has such an imposing presence, the dream shows that the emphasis should be on the aboriginal spirit of the land and what it might have to teach the white man about himself and the country; hence my decision to concentrate on the Rainbow Serpent and the medicine-man.

The image of the black and white women in the immediate foreground indicates that the attitude of both cultures toward the personal symbols of the feminine principle or anima needs to be addressed. Finally, since the outback disappears into the horizon, what follows is also about the mysterious unknown that lies beyond the horizon—the nature of the collective unconscious that we all share. It is as if we are standing there waiting to see what will emerge from an investigation of this myth.

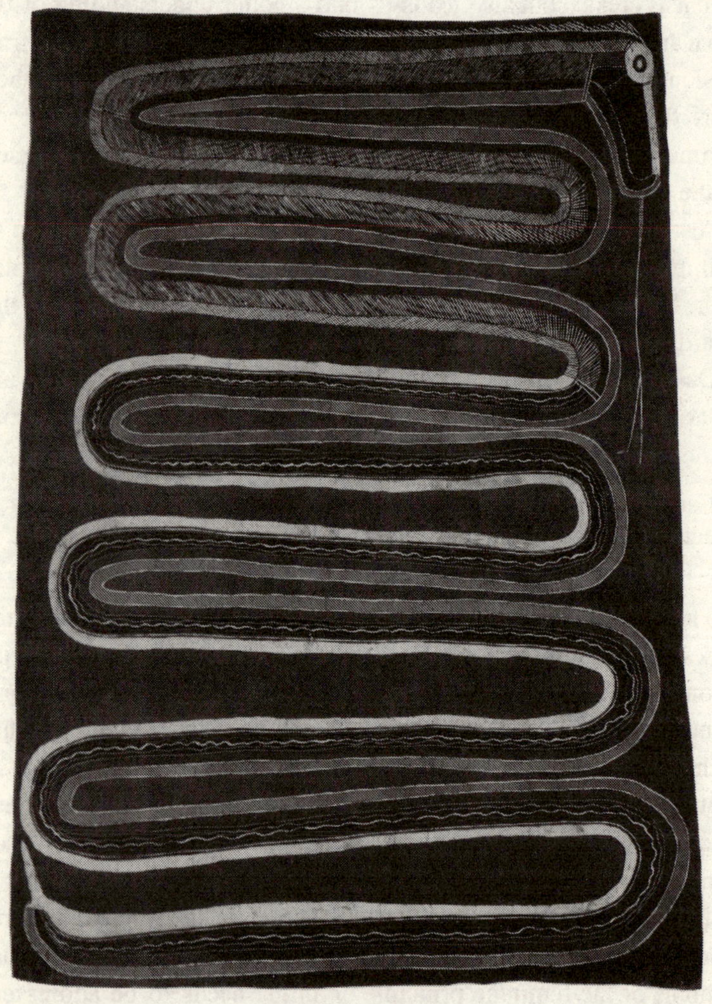

Rainbow Serpent.
(By Bargudubu, from J. Isaacs, *Australian Aboriginal Paintings*)

# 1
# The Wawilak Women

The myth of the Wawilak Women comes from an isolated and tropical part of Australia of almost exclusive aboriginal population, North-East Arnhem Land. There are two published versions of the myth, both remarkably similar even though they are from two different tribes and were recorded some thirty years apart.[1] The original source of the myth is its ritualization and each version was written after the authors were allowed to witness the ritual cycles that portray it. Our focus here will be on the Lloyd Warner version from the Murngin tribe, the first account ever recorded, in the early 1930s.

The ritual cycles have two main purposes. The primary one is to assure the fertility of earth and people as well as the perpetuation of Mother Nature's bounty, while the second is concerned with the initiation of both boys and men through various age-grading ceremonies which include the practices of circumcision and subincision. Symbolically, the fertility aspect of these rites represents a collective effort to bring the image of the Self into consciousness, while the initiation rites symbolize the process through which masculine and feminine attitudes in the psyche are centralized in an individual. Each represents a different aspect of the process of individuation.

The inspiration for the myth comes from the seasonal climatic changes that occur throughout this monsoonal region, with the wet season being a time of scarcity and the dry a time of plenty. The story is woven around these changes and in this regard it is derived from the projection of unconscious psychic contents onto the changing physical environment. Whereas fairy tales, dreams and most myths involve a projection of the unconscious into "space," our myth

---

[1] Lloyd W. Warner, *A Black Civilization: A Social Study of an Australian Tribe,* and Ronald M. Berndt, *Kunapipi: A Study of an Australian Aboriginal Religious Cult.*

comprises images that have been projected into matter. When Jung wrote, "In order to explain the mystery of matter he projected yet another mystery—his own unknown psychic background—into what was to be explained,"[2] the *he* to whom he was referring was the alchemist; however it is equally descriptive of the attempt by the Arnhem Land Aborigine to understand his fascination with the mystery of the seasons.

The unique opportunity that this myth affords, apart from its rich story, is that it comes from a people who had no contact with the outside world after arriving on the continent some 35,000 years ago. The earliest substantial contact with Europeans occurred when the first white settlement was made only some 200 years ago, in 1788, about 150 years before this myth was first recorded.

Add to this the fact that Arnhem Land is almost 2500 miles from this first settlement, and it is evident that despite the efforts of missionaries we are dealing with a people who had been minimally influenced by white culture when Warner recorded the myth. The end effect is that it contains unconscious material that has evolved without any significant influence from the type of consciousness that emerged in the Western world. We are therefore privileged to be able to examine contents of the psyche with which modern man has long since lost contact.

The main characters in the myth are the Wawilak sisters and Yurlunggur, the great snake. The form in which we meet the snake is one of many configurations of the Rainbow Serpent, a mythological character found throughout Australia. His most common form is that of a snake but he can also be found in other guises such as a crocodile, lizard or fantasy creature. His importance was noted by A.R. Radcliffe-Brown who wrote that "with some justification [the Rainbow Serpent could be] described as occupying the position of a deity."[3]

---

2 *Psychology and Alchemy*, CW 12, par. 345. [CW refers throughout to *The Collected Works of C.G. Jung*]

3 "The Rainbow Serpent in South-East Australia," p. 342.

Through the myth, we will be able to examine the qualities and powers which give him the status of a god, in addition to seeing that he is a major centralizing psychological force both for Aborigines and for other Australians seeking the true spirit of the land. It is he who will lead individuals to a reunion with the native soil of their inherited and instinctive make-up. In this regard, the myth is important for black and white alike.

## The Journey Out

At the beginning we are given a vivid description of the period or psychological setting of the myth when we are told that it derives from the mysterious realm of the collective unconscious or, in the language of the myth, Bamun.

> It was the time of Bamun (the mythological period) when Wongar men walked about and modern man had not yet appeared. Everything was different. Animals were like men then! Those two Wawilak sisters had come a long distance. They were coming from the far interior to the Arafura Sea. They had come from the far interior Kardao Kardao country. This is a clan territory of the Dua moeity. They had come from the land of the Wawilak people for Kardao Kardao is their country. The wirkul (a young woman who has not had a child) was pregnant. The gungmun (a woman who has had a child: literally, "the giver") carried her own baby under her arm in a paper-bark "cradle." It was a male child.[4]

Bamun is the Murngin term for the Dreamtime, the aboriginal creation period and a timeless state in which past, present and future events are indistinguishable. For the Aborigine the events of the original Dreamtime are as much with us today as they were in the past and will be in the future, and this phenomenon touches all facets of aboriginal life. During their rituals, for example, the actors actually become the animals, plants and mythical beings they are portraying, and actively experience the original Dreamtime. It is the same

---

[4] Extracts are from the Lloyd Warner version of the myth, except where otherwise noted. The complete text appears here in the appendix.

idea of timelessness referred to in the Bible: "Lord God Almighty, who was and is and is to come!"[5]

The notion of the Dreamtime, where the idea of an eternal force is fully accepted, accords with Jung's hypothesis that "the psychic life of the archetype is timeless."[6] This is to say that the archetype is an eternally inherited psychic form which is the basis for all experiences throughout the history of humankind and, as such, is common to all. Thus the events of this original period of creation occur in the realm of the collective unconscious, the source of all the images in the myth. It is a story about the creation of the human psyche.

The second point which shows that the myth arises from the collective unconscious is the reference to the fact that "modern man" has not yet appeared and that it is a time when animals and people are the same. In other words, there is an absence of a developed ego and rationality, and the events that follow occur in the world of the irrational, or the unconscious. They take place in chthonic nature and are the absolute counterbalance or shadow side to the principles which govern the modern world, hence the myth's relevance in compensating the psychology of twentieth-century man.

The conflict between nature and the modern world is reflected in the following dream.

> I am driving along a road when I see a wolf ahead of me. At first it begins to walk away but then turns suddenly with such a vicious look that I am terrified and stricken with panic. Then I realize that I can no longer move the car.

The dreamer was an intellectual who identified strongly with the world of consciousness. His predilection was to think through and ruminate on issues, so it is not surprising that one reason he sought analysis was to understand his constant migraines.

The car is an apt symbol of the twentieth century in that it is based on the principles of logic, precision and rationality, the dreamer's

---

[5] Revelation to John 4:8, Revised Standard Version.

[6] "Psychology and Religion," *Psychology and Religion: West and East,* CW 11, par. 149.

prevailing attitude to life. This attitude can also be seen as a collective problem, for which again the car is an appropriate metaphor in light of the large amount of energy society invests in it.[7] The wolf, on the other hand, represents the wild, nature and untamed instinct. The dream tells us that this aspect of the dreamer is demanding more of his attention. In other words his animal nature is threatening, to the point of blocking the further progress of his rational consciousness—he can no longer move the car.

In the myth, the remark that Bamun was a time when men and animals were on a par raises the dilemma Jung referred to concerning the derivation of archetypes and their relationship to instincts. He concluded that instincts and archetypes together form the collective unconscious.[8] At the same time he leaned toward the view that the instincts originally gave birth to the archetypes. This remains an unproven hypothesis, but our myth, which is essentially about the activation of the central archetype, the Self, in a chthonic environment, lends weight to the idea that the archetypes originated in the realm of the instincts—below the pool of Yurlunggur.

From another source, we know that the two sisters were the daughters of the original creator goddesses, the Djanggawul sisters, who came from the Arafura Sea off the coast of Arnhem Land.[9] Their most distinguishing features were their clitorises:

> These were so long that they dragged upon the ground as they walked. . . . The elder Sister's clitoris was the longer, while the younger Sister's was almost snakelike in appearance.[10]

As they emerged from the sea and crossed the land, their dragging

---

[7] In North America the automobile industry accounts for almost twenty-five per cent of all income generated in the manufacturing sector, while some twenty per cent of personal income is allocated to the running of a car. *Census of Manufacturers, 1988; Car Costs, 1990,* Canadian Automobile Association.

[8] "Instinct and the Unconscious," *The Structure and Dynamics of the Psyche,* CW 8, pars. 263-270.

[9] R. M. Berndt, *Djanggawul,* p. xvii.

[10] Ibid., pp. 24-25.

clitorises formed the river beds.[11] Thus the Djanggawuls provided the tracts along which the water of life could flow. In psychological terms, they made it possible for psychic energy to be exchanged between the unconscious (sea) and the ego (land).

The rivers in this area can flow in either direction depending on the season; fresh water flows to the sea during the wet season, and salt water flows from the sea during the dry. In other words, the Djanggawuls created a system in which energy could flow to and from the unconscious and the ego complex, a dynamic that is essential for the creation of consciousness. Jung referred to the directed flow of psychic energy as the "canalization of libido," which he described as a process of "energic transformation or conversion" and a "transfer of psychic intensities or values from one content to another."[12] The sisters in the Djanggawul myth provided the psychic infrastructure through which man could progress from instinctual bondage to the development of cultural values.

For example, in a child's development libido is initially centered in the nutritional and erogenous zones. Jung observed that later in life energy naturally moves in other directions. This is the basis of the urge for individuation, a process reflected in the myth where the basic instincts are eventually channeled into the river bed, the waters of the Rainbow Serpent. For the Murngin the canalization of energy was made possible through the actions of the Djanggawuls, and without them all life would have remained in the great womb of the unconscious, the Arafura Sea. In much the same way, Adam and Eve would have remained in the Garden of Eden had not the snake led them away from their blissful and passive life.

Although regarded as female, the sisters' pronounced clitorises suggest a prominent masculine feature; that is, they have hermaphroditic characteristics. This is typical of figures encountered in dreams when a person needs to develop his or her contrasexual nature.

---

11 Warner, *Black Civilization*, p. 346.

12 "On Psychic Energy," *The Structure and Dynamics of the Psyche*, CW 8, par. 79.

One woman dreamt of herself with an exaggerated penis and wanting to make love to a woman who looked like herself. The dreamer was an artist with an acknowledged world-class talent, but her creativity was crippled by an undeveloped masculine side. The result was that she allowed the men in her life to control the way she expressed herself artistically. The dream compensates her conscious attitude and directs her to develop her own masculine strength rather than rely on male authority figures to tell her what to do. In a similar vein the myth demonstrates how the land, the feminine element, must be fertilized by the masculine quality of mother nature (the "penises" of the Djanggawuls) if energy is to flow.

The Djanggawuls came from the chaos of the Arafura Sea, the "home of the *dua* moeity dead,"[13] symbolic of a primeval and undifferentiated state of the psyche. Interestingly, the phrase "house of the dead" was used by medieval alchemists to denote the place of origin of their *prima materia,* the original substance of their work, to which a bisexual quality was ascribed.[14]

The sexual identity of the Wawilaks is not as confused as that of the Djanggawuls; rather they represent the differentiated feminine side of their mothers. They are not androgynous but instinctual feminine figures.

The Djanggawuls are the true creator goddesses, forming the land features and producing all the plants and animals as well as the prototypes of the first people. In addition they established the social structure which is patrilineal in that the marriage system is determined by the father's lineage. The unconscious forces in the aboriginal psyche are represented by the feminine principle. For both the Djanggawuls and the Wawilaks the role of men is relatively unimportant, if not insignificant. We are told very little about their male consorts who, like their children, do not warrant a name and do not play an active role in the respective myths.

---

[13] Berndt, *Djanggawul,* p. 24.

[14] Jung, *Alchemy: Notes on Lectures Given at the Eidgenössische Technische Hochschule, Zurich* (summer semester, 1941), p. 97.

In fact, the whole story is played out within the broad attitude of the feminine, even when the masculine snake appears, because the Dua moeity which owns the myth is feminine, having been established by the Djanggawuls. By contrast the opposing moeity, the Yiritja, was established by their arch rival, Laintjung, who is male and whose moeity is considered to be inferior to the Dua which inherited the responsibility for all the important rituals. And so, during their travels, the Wawilaks are very careful not to enter masculine territory—"they never walked on the country of the Yiritja moeity."

## Women on the Move

The two women carried stone spears and hawks' down and bush cotton. On the way they killed iguana, opossum, and bandicoot for their food. They also gathered some bush yams (ippa). When they killed the animals, they gave them the names they bear today; they did the same for the yam. They gathered all the plants and animals that are in the Murngin country today. They said to each thing they killed or gathered, "You will be maraiin [a totemic emblem] by and by."

When the two sisters started their journey they talked Djaun, later Rainbarngo, and still later Djinba; then they talked Wawilak, and finally Liaalaomir. They named the country as they went along. In the Wawilak country they copulated with Wawilak Wongar men. These men were Dua, and they were Dua. This was very wrong and asocial.

The two women stopped to rest, for the younger felt the child she was carrying move inside her. She knew her baby would soon be born.

"Yeppa [sister], I feel near my heart this baby turning," she said.

The older one said, "Then let us rest."

They sat down, and the older sister put her hand on the abdomen of the younger sister and felt the child moving inside. She then massaged her younger sister, for she knew the labour pains had commenced. The baby was born there. It was Yiritja, for its mother was Dua. The country was still a part of the territory of the Wawilak clan.

After the child was born the older sister gathered more bush food, then the two moved on toward the sea. They stopped at various places and gave all of them names. They named all the clan territories and the localities within their borders. They first rested at Djirri Djirri (quail place), then at Wakngay (crow place), Dung Dunga (fish spear place), Tarbella (white oyster place), and Katatanga (falling meteor place). All these localities were Dua and were within the country of the Wawilak clan. Although the Wawilak sisters went to almost all the clans of the Dua moeity they never walked on the country of the Yiritja moeity.

"Come on, sister," said the older, "we'll go quickly now." They drank water at the last place and hurried on. . . .

They did not stop until they sat down at the great Mirrirmina (rock python's back) water hole in the country of the Liaalaomir clan. It is in the bottom of this well in the deep subterranean waters below the upper waters that Yurlunggur, the great copper snake, or python totem of the Dua moeity, lives. They called the country for the first time Mirrirmina.

The older sister took her fire drill and made a fire. She started cooking the all yams and other bush food that she had gathered and all the animals that they had killed on their journey.

"Sister, you cook my food for me, too," said the younger one.

We are not told why the two sisters are compelled to move, we are only told they are undertaking a journey from the bush to the Arafura Sea—from one unknown to another. However, we already know that the Arafura Sea is the home of the original creator goddesses, and it is to this chaos that they would be reverting if they were to reach their destination. In other words, their libido is seeking a reunion with the Djanggawuls, the parental imagoes. Should the sisters be successful they would become enmeshed in the dark *prima materia* of their beginning, a time when there was no consciousness. Psychologically, therefore, the movement starts as a regression; the psychic energy is seeking the all-embracing, possessive nature of the parental imagoes. This means they would be moving from a state where feminine consciousness was slightly differentiated to a state of androgynous confusion.

This raises a motif that appears throughout the myth and is the basis for aboriginal kinship laws, the motif of incest. Incest is a privilege normally reserved for the gods, whom the Wawilaks are. However the other side to godly incest is practiced by animals who have no incest taboo. In fact the better breeds of animals result from highly incestuous unions. Since our story takes place during a time when "animals were like men," it follows that the Wawilaks originate in this other side. They become pregnant unconsciously and indiscriminately through unions with relatives.

Up to this point, the Wawilaks are incapable of discrimination because they lack the masculine principle or Logos which would give them this ability. They give the impression that they will commune with anyone. The result is that they cannot enter a conscious relationship with their consorts because Eros is caught in the web of instinctual desire. Before they can acquaint themselves with the essential masculine side of their personalities, their desires will require more refining and greater consciousness.

In this regard the Wawilak sisters can be seen as caught in the desire to return to the complex of the parents. They themselves, after all, are only one step removed from the completely undifferentiated state of the mothers. Their incest derives from kinship libido, designed to hold the family together. More specifically, they are seeking reunion with the masculine side of the Djanggawuls. The effect of following this tendency is to stay psychologically within the family complex, repeating past patterns of family history and having them dominate conscious life. And so, when the Wawilaks get the urge to head off to the Arafura Sea, they are guilty of the urge to dissolve their burgeoning consciousness in the unconsciousness of the family. This is a regressive path.

In an individual's psychology this would be equivalent to one's unique characteristics being buried under traditional collective attitudes. The ability to form personal relationships, develop true feeling responses and be receptive to new possibilities would be reduced to an interest in object relations, cold purpose and single-minded endeavor. One's true nature would not be experienced.

In terms of the myth, the land would remain unproductive and human procreation would cease, because producing off-spring from an incestuous union is not allowed under tribal law. There would be no young boys to be initiated into the secrets of the tribe.

Paradoxically, it is the very desire of the Wawilaks to seek the comfort of their parents that activates their journey on the path of individuation. Their relationship to the animals and the transformation of the animals through acts of killing, naming and cooking is integral to the Wawilaks' role of leading both themselves and the great snake into consciousness.

The animals represent the untamed libido of the Wawilaks. It is far from consciousness, lodged in the chthonic realm of the instincts. As long as there is no awareness of this instinctual energy, the Wawilaks run the risk of being unconsciously controlled by it.

An animal's power is not really its own, it belongs to nature. It is this raw instinctual quality that both controls the lives of the Wawilaks and is later transformed by them and brought into the service of the great snake. In other words, through the urge to individuate, the archetypal world of Yurlunggur will be discovered. Because the anima figures deal with their instinctual nature and eventually act in a preeminently conscious manner toward it, they begin the process of releasing their unrealized psychic energy.

The Wawilaks give names to the animals. From a psychological perspective, naming represents a decisive act. In this sense, it is indicative of masculine Logos. It is as if the Wawilaks came to an intuitive decision that they needed a clearer focus if they were to get out of their current state of wandering. So they set about clearly identifying the objects around them. Through the focused act of naming, they escape the grip of pure nature.

At the same time, the effect of giving a name to something is to invest that object with power. To the primitive mind this power is magical, fascinating. According to Jung this is also a quality of the archetypes.[15] One could say that the Wawilaks are involved in a process by which the symbolic, archetypal aspect of the natural world is recognized as part of humanity's psychic system and not the exclu-

---

15 "One can perceive the specific energy of the archetypes when one experiences the peculiar feeling of numinosity that accompanies them—the fascination or spell that emanates from them." ("Symbols and the Interpretation of Dreams," *The Symbolic Life,* CW 18, par. 547)

sive property of untamed nature.

In Berndt's version of the myth, after naming the animals the two sisters kill them and put them in dilly bags.[16] Thus they overtly take action and sacrifice the instinctual or undifferentiated aspect of themselves, the same aspect that led them to regress. Their forward striving libido is now able to separate from the parents. As a result they are destined never to reach the Arafura Sea.

At this point it would appear that the Wawilaks have lost their urge to reenter the world of the parents. They know what they don't want, but not what they want. They suffer in their dilemma and this causes their emotions and feelings to be aroused. Heat is associated with the generation of emotions, and it is this that becomes the source of the fire through which their instincts are cooked and transformed.

Making fire is a preeminent act of consciousness. For the primitive it is also a traditional method of making a sacrifice to the gods and as such provides a continuing link between the human and the divine. In other words it is through the act of cooking that the instincts of the Wawilaks are transformed from the chthonic material realm into another form. Whereas their energy had previously been directed by an urge back toward the unconscious, it is now directed toward their inner nourishment and development. The chthonic libido has been sacrificed, that is, made sacred, allowing the material world of the instincts to meet the spiritual world of the archetypes.

Among the Aborigines dilly bags are hung from the waist and sometimes referred to as the "uterus." Coincidentally, the *vas hermeticum* of the alchemists was also called, among other names, the uterus and was the vessel in which the *prima materia* was cooked. The object was to purify and refine the steam to such an extent that the pneuma or spiritus would reach the highest degree of subtlety.[17]

In effect, this is exactly what the Wawilaks did. The psychological result of their cooking ceremony was that the purified animal spirits

---

[16] *Kunapipi*, p. 20

[17] Jung, *Alchemy: Notes on Lectures Given at the Eidgenössische Technische Hochschule, Zurich* (winter semester, 1940-41), p. 86.

were released. No longer would their Eros express itself in purely sexual terms. Their instinctual nature entered the pool of the snake transformed, no longer limited to the cycle of incest.

A further comparison can be made with the *calcinatio* fire operation in alchemy, symbolically related to the purging of purely physical desire. Edward Edinger writes that "the *calcinatio* is performed on the primitive shadow side, which harbors hungry, instinctual desirousness and is contaminated by the unconscious."[18] In like manner did the Wawilaks purge the dark side of their natural instincts by cooking the yams and leaving only the ash.[19]

The notion of cooking is also relevant to what happens in the analytic process, where aspects of the shadow are "sweated out."

The eventual question to be asked is what these drives want of an individual. In the myth this question is answered by the transformed spirits of the animals when they immediately jump from the fire and run into the black well of Yurlunggur.

> As soon as they cooked the food each animal and plant jumped out of the fire and ran to the Mirrirmina water hole and jumped into it. They all went into this Djungguan and Gunabibi well. The crab ran in first. When he did this, the two women talked Liaalaomir for the first time; before this they had talked Wawilak. The other plants and animals followed the crab. The yams ran like men, as did the iguanas, frill-neck lizard, darpa, ovarku snake, rock python, sea gull, sea eagles, native companion and crocodiles. Each ran and dived into the clans' totemic well and disappeared from sight.

The result of the animals and plants jumping into the pool is that a connection is made between the two sisters and the great Rainbow Serpent via the spirit. By gathering, killing, naming and cooking, they are able to enter into a relationship with the deep unconscious, the sleeping Yurlunggur. Whereas they had been seeking incestuous relations with the parental imagoes, they now begin a dialogue with the archetype of the father, the great masculine deity.

---

[18] *Anatomy of the Psyche: Alchemical Symbolism in Psychotherapy*, pp. 21-22.
[19] Berndt, *Kunapipi*, p. 22.

This archetypal pattern is reflected in the personal situation facing a young woman raised in a "good" Catholic family which recognized only the light side of God. It became her fate to have to deal with the dark side and this had led her into a depression. In particular it was the father principle which was problematic and her libido had been seeking the father. This was graphically portrayed in a dream where she had an incestuous union with him. This woman had a deeply religious attitude to life and was struggling to find her own personal relationship with the godhead. Her dreams were highly religious and showed where the libido that was trapped by her depression was most active. In one dream she was with a "type of grandfather." She watched him perform a ritual which involved the burning or sacrificing of animals. From the fire emerged "spectral colors."

There is a parallel with the Wawilak myth. The woman's upbringing had suppressed her sexual energies, which remained unconsciously tied to her father; the grandfather dream introduces the motif of refining these instincts in much the same way as the Wawilaks refined theirs. Before her true religious energies could be brought to consciousness, her dark shadow, archaic and chthonic, had to be refined. In the dream the *calcinatio* is performed by a grandfather figure (Great Father) who converts her animal nature to a spiritual form, symbolized by the spectral colors. Similarly, one of the alchemists' aims was to create the "colours of the *peacock's eye,*" or *cauda pavonis,* symbol of the coveted *lapis.*[20]

The dream shows that the goal her libido seeks is not the personal father but the godhead. In like manner the refined animal spirits of the Wawilaks sought the multicolored Rainbow Serpent or *lapis* in the pool.

Together with the animal spirits, the sister's blood also finds its way to the domain of Yurlunggur. Specifically, the source of the blood is the menses, the blood discarded by a woman's body when her womb has not been fertilized.

---

[20] "A Study in the Process of Individuation," *The Archetypes and the Collective Unconscious,* CW 9i, par. 580.

The older woman went out to gather bark to make a bed for her sister's baby after it was born. She walked over some of the water of the Mirrirmina well. Her menstrual blood fell in the totem well and was carried down the sacred water hole, where Yurlunggur, the Big Father, lives.

When menstrual blood dropped into the pool Yurlunggur smelled the odor of this pollution from where he was lying in the black water beneath the floor of the totem well. His head was lying quietly on the bottom of the pit. He raised his head and smelled again and again.

"Where does this blood come from?" he said. He opened the bottom of the well by throwing the stone which covers its base out of the well on to the land by the women's camp.

The menstrual blood symbolizes a potential for creativity, which in the myth previously had been channeled into incest. Now it is available for use elsewhere in the psychic system, namely to awaken the great snake, the unconscious masculine principle.

This process is reflected in a dream a man had while going through a psychological crisis. As so often happens when one is stuck in a stressful situation, the unconscious produced an archetypal image. In the dream he was looking into a toilet bowl which was filled with blood, pieces of flesh and perhaps sperm. Something caught his eye and he fished it out; it was a little man about eight inches tall. His aunt was with him and said it would live.

As in alchemy, the dreamer has his *soror mystica,* female assistant, in the person of his aunt—an aspect of his anima—to help him in the opus. The dream indicates that it is from base materials that the "treasure hard to attain" will emerge. For the dreamer this meant he would have to come to terms with unpleasant contents of his shadow. The representation of the treasure as a little man is analogous to the alchemical "little metal man"[21] or *spiritus metallorum,*[22] and "pissing manikin,"[23] which along with dwarfs, elves and Tom

---

[21] "The Psychology of the Child Archetype," *The Archetypes and the Collective Unconscious,* CW 9i, par. 268.

[22] *Psychology and Alchemy,* CW 12, par. 40.

[23] Ibid., fig. 121.

Thumbs symbolize hidden forces of nature.

More particularly, in alchemy the little man is commonly the figure Mercurius, creative divinity of the opus and, as we shall see, closely related symbolically to Yurlunggur, the Rainbow Serpent. Significantly, in the dream the little man emerges from the vessel (the toilet bowl) which contains flesh and blood, just as the *lapis* "grows from flesh and blood."[24]

The alchemists' search for the philosophical gold in the most base of materials fits well with the myth where we are told that the menstrual blood has an unpleasantness to it: "the odour of . . . pollution." Also, for the alchemists, blood in the form of the "red tincture" expressed "the healing or whole-making effect of a certain kind of Eros."[25] In short, blood represents a feeling value able to bridge opposites, which in our myth are the Wawilak women and Yurlunggur.

For the primitive, blood is a symbol for the soul as well as being the essence of humanity.[26] Through the blood in the well, the masculine Yurlunggur receives a feminine soul. Similarly, according to the alchemists, the soul or *anima corporalis*[27] of the *lapis* was in the blood. In terms of an individual's psychology, the image presented is that of Eros entering the divine waters and animating the unconscious. The snake, meanwhile, receives a double benefit: the refined spirit derived from the transformed instincts, as well as the blood which contains the soul. In this way the Wawilaks' instinctual libido is transformed and directed toward the unconscious where contact is made with the masculine.

The connection with Yurlunggur is first made in the well. Though it is a more contained area of the unconscious than the chaos of the sea the sisters had set out to find, it still represents the unconscious and Yurlunggur is himself unconscious.

Yurlunggur is found in a state of inertia, his head lying quietly in

---

24 Ibid., par. 243.

25 "The Philosophical Tree," *Alchemical Studies,* CW 13, par. 390.

26 "Paracelsus and the Spiritual Phenomenon," ibid., par. 180.

27 *Psychology and Alchemy,* CW 12, par. 397.

the black water. In many primitive traditions the head represents the place where the spirit lies, suggesting that here the spirit is dormant. The description of Yurlunggur is one of nature incarnate, at rest and in a state of perfect balance but at the same time stagnating. Whereas the instincts (animals-Wawilaks) are associated with action, here we find a figure with no active life of its own. In this sense he represents the essence of an archetype, which Jung describes as "systems of readiness for action . . . the chthonic portion of the psyche, that portion of the psyche that is attached to nature."[28]

The image of Yurlunggur at the bottom of the well is thus one of nature inchoate, with only the potential for action. In terms of Christian mythology, this is a picture reminiscent of Paradise before the Fall, a state in which mankind would have remained had Adam and Eve not been tempted out of the garden.

According to Jung, immersion in the bath or well represents a descent into the unconscious, a kind of "night sea journey."[29] It can also symbolize the potential for rebirth.[30] Jung observed that the alchemists seemed to be trying to demonstrate that the unconscious itself initiates the process of renewal.[31] This possibility is also suggested in our myth, for it is the Wawilaks' spontaneous unconscious actions that lead to Yurlunggur's emergence from the well.

Here we get closer to the psychological meaning behind the myth. It is about the emergence of the Self in a form that can be personally experienced, through the rituals and initiation ceremonies of the Murngin. Without the intervention of the Wawilaks, who represent Eros, the Murngin would not have been led to a knowledge of this supreme being. Part of the Self would have remained sleeping in the cold, deep unconscious. Like the archetypal figure that he is, Yurlunggur becomes the form that the instincts assume—a self-por-

---

[28] "Mind and Earth," *Civilization in Transition,* CW 10, par. 53.

[29] "The Psychology of the Transference," *The Practice of Psychotherapy,* CW 16, par. 455.

[30] See Marie-Louise von Franz, *Redemption Motifs in Fairytales,* pp. 21ff.

[31] "The Psychology of the Transference," *The Practice of Psychotherapy,* CW 16, pars. 458ff.

trait of the instincts.[32] He will emerge because he receives both spirit and soul. Yurlunggur feels the urge to enter life. "Where does this blood come from?" he asks. As we shall see in the next chapter, asking the right question is a common motif in the development of consciousness.

And so the Rainbow Serpent is disturbed and begins to stir. The Wawilaks become aware of a power greater than themselves, just as an individual may realize that the ego is not the center of the psyche.

Until the blood and the animals entered the pool, Yurlunggur was dormant, a mere possibility. Once animated, he begins to take some initiative. His first action is to remove the stone from the well. In so doing he removes the barrier between the upper or more personal levels of the unconscious, in which the Wawilaks had been living, and the lower level, the collective unconscious, where the ultimate value will be found. In alchemical terms, he reveals to the sisters "a sealed up treasure, which God only opens for the chosen,"[33] and allows himself the opportunity to directly experience life.

---

[32] "Instinct and the Unconscious," *The Structure and Dynamics of the Psyche,* CW 8, par. 277.

[33] Djabir (eighth-century alchemist), in Berthelot, *La Chimie au Moyen-Age,* vol. 3, p. 188..

# 2

# The Serpent Shows His Colors

Until the blood entered the well the masculine and feminine principles were hermetically sealed off from one another. For the Wawilak sisters their world was the dry "far interior Kardao Kardao country," which represents not only natural and instinctual life but also the body. By contrast Yurlunggur's world was one of water, corresponding to the alchemists' "radical moisture," believed to contain the spirit or pneuma.[1]

## Meeting Yurlunggur

> He crawled out slowly, like a snake does, from the well. When he came out he sucked some of the well water into his mouth. He spat it into the sky. Soon a cloud about the size of a man's hand appeared from nowhere in the center of the sky. As Yurlunggur slowly rose from out of the bottom of the pool the totemic well water rose too and flooded the earth. He pulled himself up on the stone which he had thrown, and laid his head there. He looked around him. He saw the women and their babies. Yurlunggur was older brother to these women, and they were sisters to him. Their children were his wakus, and he was gawel to them.

Yurlunggur begins his journey by slowly crawling out of the black water, stating that his purpose is to find the source of the blood. In other words his intention is to leave a primeval state of unconsciousness. He announces his arrival by spitting out water from the well into the sky, forming a cloud that takes up a central position. This is the sign of a god with supreme powers.

By showing that he rules the world of water, Yurlunggur establishes not only that he comes from the deep unconscious but also that

---

[1] "The Visions of Zosimos," *Alchemical Studies*, CW 13, par. 89.

he is the key to the level of prevailing unconsciousness through his ability to control the level of the flood. His mastery over water demonstrates that he possesses archetypal qualities and, in this context, is comparable to Mercurius, spirit of the unconscious.[2]

The implication of this show of power for an individual is that one must establish an active relationship with the great snake—the unconscious—if he is not to turn destructive. Like Mercurius, he will not harm the person who has the right attitude and seeks an active relationship with him. On the other hand, through tricks or other spontaneous expressions of the unconscious, he will wreak havoc on the person with the wrong attitude. He will allow the flood to rise and the power of it to be felt by the person trying to live without recognizing his presence. In individual psychology, the clear danger is that of being overwhelmed by the unconscious and losing all ego involvement in life.

It is in the spirit of demanding that the Wawilaks recognize his symbolic value that Yurlunggur delivers the flood and forcibly draws their attention to the one-sided nature of their lives. It seems that his motivation is much the same as Jahweh's in the Biblical myth; just as Jahweh flooded the world when it became degenerate and wicked, so Yurlunggur sends forth a flood in response to the "crimes" committed by the Wawilaks, namely their incestuous deeds stemming from the desire to return to the chaotic world of the parents. The threatening flood is a strong message from the unconscious to change their ego standpoint. Yurlunggur reduces the whole world to its *prima materia;* the old ego attitudes are washed away and the opportunity is created for a new attitude to be born.

It is as if Yurlunggur had initiated an alchemical process whereby, through a process of washing or *solutio,*[3] only those aspects of the personality that are related to the Self can survive, and a transformation of the individual becomes possible.

---

[2] See "The Spirit Mercurius," ibid., pars. 239ff.

[3] See Edward F. Edinger, *Anatomy of the Psyche: Alchemical Symbolism in Psychotherapy,* chapt. 3.

The perceived threat from the movement of the great snake is too much for the Wawilaks. They do everything in their power to avoid a confrontation with the unconscious.

> Yurlunggur continued to look at them. He hissed. This was to call out for rain. There was no cloud in the sky until then, but soon the two sisters saw a small, a very small, black cloud appear in the heavens. They did not see the great python lying there watching them.
>
> The cloud grew larger and larger, and soon the rain came down. The Wawilak sisters hurriedly built a house to be ready for the rain. They named the forked sticks they used as uprights. The women went inside the house. They did not know where this rain came from; they did not know that the older sister's menstrual blood had defiled the Mirrirmina water hole and had made Yurlunggur angry.
>
> The Wawilak women went to sleep, but the rain poured down harder and harder and awakened them.

The sisters' first reaction to the call of the unconscious is to build a house to avoid the thundering rain, which represents the voice and sign of this inner figure demanding attention. Up to this point their actions have been mainly extraverted, in that their libido has generally flowed toward the outer world.[4] They killed and cooked the animals and named the objects in their environment which, for the primitive, is equivalent to having power over that object. Power is an aspect of extraversion. Now Yurlunggur's fearful presence prompts them to go inside, which would indicate that he forces them to introvert. For the first time, they find themselves in a situation where they feel that the energy coming from the object will overwhelm them. Thus there is a change in the flow of their energy that is characteristic of an introverted attitude.

This is what commonly happens to a person following an experience of the unconscious. It is as if, by realizing a presence greater than one's own ego, one moves from the first half of life, usually dominated by extraverted values, to the second half where one's primary task is the inner journey.

---

[4] *Psychological Types,* CW 6, pars. 330ff.

This theme is reflected in the case of a man who had been successful in his career but had lost the zest not only for his job but also for life in general. In the midst of a determined search to find out where his energy wanted to take him he had a dream.

> I see an image of a cross. Then I am in a desert where I am sitting in a small, simple shack filled with rich warm sunlight. Next to me is an aboriginal woman. Jung enters the room and says I will no longer need my clothes. He hands me a block of iron and tells me to do something with it.
>
> Then I see that the woman has her hand down the throat of a very large and colorful snake, but she does not seem frightened. Later she gives me a tie of snake skin that she says will provide protection from any imaginable threat.

The dreamer knew nothing of our myth nor of the Rainbow Serpent, yet clearly the unconscious presents a number of similar motifs—a testament to the archetypal world we all share. First there is a cross, associated with Christianity, an extraverted and patriarchal religion. Psychologically the cross is also a symbol of conflict, which here, in light of the dreamer's situation, pertains to an inner struggle to reconcile traditional collective values—the patriarchal world of success, power and money—with his own personal needs.

We will return to this dream later, but for now it is enough to note that Jung directs him not only to get rid of his old attitudes (his clothes), but also to work with a dark metal.

Jung wrote extensively about the symbolic meaning of alchemy, an art involving the "transmutation of the elements," closely associated with the mythology and legends of the smelting of iron.[5] Through the dreamer's associations, it seemed that Jung was directing him to acquaint himself with this ancient art. The symbols that arise in the opus would presumably be a means for the dreamer to work through his depression (the black metal). Further analysis

---

[5] "On Psychic Energy," *The Structure and Dynamics of the Psyche*, CW 8, par. 90; see also Mircea Eliade, *The Forge and the Crucible*, pp. 27ff.

showed that he would also benefit from an attempt to understand the world of nature, the feminine principle. That the action of the dream takes place in a simple hut suggests that the dreamer's energy should be directed inward, a focus commonly associated, as already mentioned, with the second half of life.

The initial attempt by the snake to attract the Wawilaks is in vain. Huddled together in the house, they remain unaware of the source of the rain. Nonetheless, they see the dark and threatening cloud hanging directly above.

The black cloud symbolizes depression, a heaviness of spirit, a state familiar to the alchemists as the *nigredo* stage of the opus— "melancholia, 'a black blacker than black,' night, an affliction of the soul, confusion, etc., or, more pointedly, the 'black raven.' "[6] In the context of the myth, it is symptomatic of the sisters' need to do something. The dark cloud belongs to their inner life; their energy has been forced into the inner sanctum, confined there by the overwhelming power of the snake.

The Wawilaks' libido is stuck, depressed by the complex they have yet to come to terms with. Their reaction to the threat is to fall asleep—become unconscious—but this cannot last long because the message from Yurlunggur, expressed through the thundering rain, is so strong that it forces them awake.

Jolted out of their innocent state, they question the source of the rain, essentially a religious question, indicating their dawning awareness of a spiritual dimension to life. This comes after receiving the fertilizing rains from the heavens; the moisture of Yurlunggur has fertilized the earth of the Wawilaks.

> The gungmun said, "Sister, where does this rain come from? There's no cloud in the north or south, and there is no cloud in the east or west, but over us is this huge black cloud. I think something is wrong. I think something terrible is going to happen."
> She got up and went outside. The younger one stayed within the

---

6 "Tractatus aureus," *Ars chemica,* p. 12 (quoted by Jung in *Mysterium Coniunctionis,* CW 14, par. 37).

house and sang. The gungmun beat the ground with her yam stick; she knew now that Yurlunggur was going to swallow her, and she wanted to stop the rain. She sang, "Yurlunggur, don't you come out and swallow us. We are good, and we are clean." While she sang she danced around the house. The two sisters then called out the taboo names of the Mirrirmina well.

Just as Yurlunggur had asked, "Where does this blood come from?" now the Wawilaks ask, "Where does this rain come from?"

The motif of having to ask the right question before the fortunes of a prevailing situation can change also appears in the Grail legend. The failure of Perceval to ask the right question meant that the existing state of the nation would continue—the fisher-king would remain sick and the surrounding country would remain unproductive. Just so would the land of the Murngin remain infertile unless the masculine and feminine principles entered into a permanent and conscious relationship. For Perceval, finally asking the right question resulted in the king regaining his health, the land becoming fertile again, and Perceval eventually becoming the guardian of the Holy Grail; that is, he developed a permanent relationship with the soul of the godhead. The redeeming question was: "Who is served from the Grail?" or, "To whom is the Grail brought?"[7]

These are questions which really mean, "How can I serve the Self?" rather than, "What can the Self do for me?" It is the same type of far-reaching question that the rumblings of Yurlunggur force the Wawilaks to ask. By questioning the source of the rain they are acknowledging that there may be a force greater than their own will.

After experiencing the strength of this greater presence they become frightened and plead their case. They claim that because they are good and clean, they should be saved. In effect they make the traditional Christian argument that because they have been good servants, obeyed all the collective laws and done what the higher authorities have expected of them, they should be saved from unpleasantness. They imagine that a one-sided, pure nature should be

---

[7] Emma Jung and Marie-Louise von Franz, *The Grail Legend,* p. 295.

enough to excuse them from having to deal with the dark or unknown side of life, where the real religious experience lies in wait.

For Yurlunggur, their plea is not good enough and he continues on his mission to fully confront them with his powerful presence. The Wawilaks are destined to meet the unknown side of their own nature, which in this case is the frightening presence of a god. The religious problem could not be willed away.

> While the older sister sang and danced around the house, and the younger sister sang inside it to stop the rain coming down and to drive the great cloud away, they were being surrounded by all the snakes in the land. The pythons, death adders, tree snakes, black snakes, tiger snakes, iguanas, the blue-tongued lizard, snails, caterpillars, and all the Dua snakes came up around them in a circle, for they had heard the call of their father, Yurlunggur. It was night and the women did not see them.

In order to strengthen the power of the signs he has been sending, Yurlunggur calls on the many facets of his primal nature to surround the two sisters. These are all primitive animals with which it is impossible to have a human relationship. They represent the sheer instinctual psyche. In such a confrontation it is impossible to manipulate the situation by will power. The multiplication of Yurlunggur's image also indicates that he is approaching the threshold of their consciousness, just on the verge of appearing.

However the Wawilaks continue to resist. In individual psychology this is comparable to what often happens when one first experiences the unconscious: it is so frightening that it constellates negative and defensive attitudes.

> The gungmun first sang all the songs sung in the general camp during Gunabibi. These are the less powerful songs. She did this first, for she thought they would stop the rain, but it did not stop. She was afraid of this rain, for it came out of a cloud she could not understand, because this cloud had come from nowhere.
> She sang then the taboo songs of the Djungguan. . . .
> The rain continued and came down harder and harder. They decided that they must sing something even more powerful, more taboo, and deeper within the ceremonial camp of the men.

Initially the Wawilaks sing the general songs which are for all ears including women and the uninitiated men, but as their fear increases they sing the more sacred songs of both the Dua and Yiritja moeities. This means they are forced into a deeper psychological journey where they are not only inspired to sing from the feminine side (Dua), but also from the masculine (Yiritja). Thus they experience the double nature of their psyche for the first time. Singing is also associated with emotion, the result of a "feeling-toned complex."[8] This suggests that the key to the women embarking on the rest of their journey is a complex Yurlunggur was able to constellate, namely the religious complex.

## Moving Inward

They sang Yurlunggur and menstrual blood.
　　When Yurlunggur heard these words, he crawled into the camp of the two women and their two children. They had suddenly fallen into a deep sleep from his magic. He licked the women and children all over preparatory to swallowing them. He bit the noses of each and made the blood come. He swallowed the old woman first, the wirkul next, and the little boys last.
　　He waited for daylight. When dawn came he uncoiled and went out a short distance in the bush, because he was too near the water. He wanted to leave the women in a dry place.

The women are asleep as Yurlunggur penetrates their camp. He symbolically enters, and becomes an integral part of, the Wawilak psyche. He is no longer an autonomous complex.

The ritualization of this part of the myth is expressed in overt sexual actions and is interpreted by the Murngin as simply representing "penis in vagina."[9] This is more less accepted by most anthropologists writing on the myth,[10] but Róheim extends this interpretation,

---

8 "A Review of the Complex Theory," *The Structure and Dynamics of the Psyche,* CW 8, pars. 194ff.

9 Berndt, *Kunapipi,* p. 25.

10 Ibid., pp. 12, 31; Warner, *A Black Civilization,* pp. 371-386; C. Lévi-Strauss, *The Savage Mind,* p. 93.

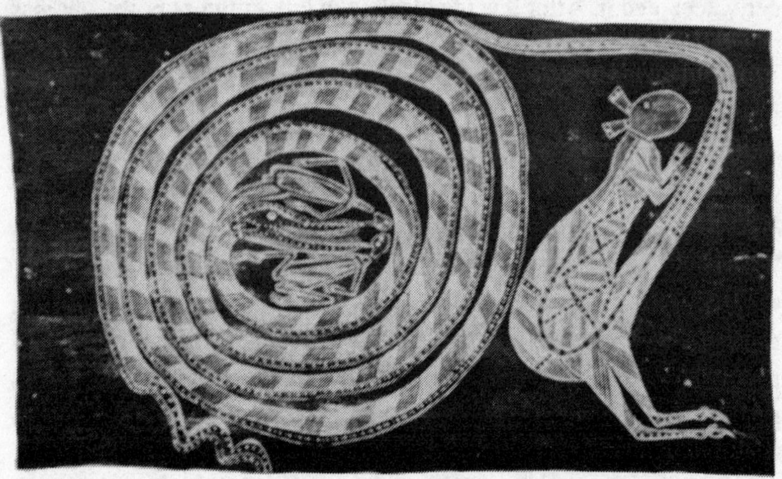

Aboriginal bark painting from Arnhem Land showing the two
sisters being swallowed by the Rainbow Serpent.
(From Francis Huxley, *The Way of the Sacred*)

seeing the events in purely Freudian terms, as wish-fulfillment.[11]
The snake-penis enters the female camp-uterus, sprays them with
saliva or *ngal* [12] (the word the Murngin use for both spit and sperm)
and consummates the sexual union unconsciously wished for.

Similar images appeared in the dream of a man who was confronted with completing a creative task he had been working on for
some time. Its final completion was being held back by his nervous-
ness about submitting his work to public scrutiny. His dream involved a test which would be performed by a black man. It was first
carried out on the dreamer's two teen-age daughters, the black man
delivering a stream of spittle from his mouth into theirs. The girls
squirmed and were reluctant to receive it. The dreamer, however, ea-

---

[11] "Snakes stand erect, and thus represent phallos in erection; but they also
swallow beings, and thus typify fantasies and anxieties connected with
vagina and uterus." (G. Róheim, *The Eternal Ones of the Dream: A Psychoanalytic Interpretation of Australian Myth and Ritual*, p. 196)
[12] Berndt, *Kunapipi*, p. 25.

gerly accepted it. After this the black man left, cutting his way across the countryside.

Clearly the spittle-sperm is invading the space of two young women reluctant to receive it. An interpretation from a Freudian perspective might suggest that the father is merely carrying out the incest wish he secretly has for his daughters; however there is more to this dream than wish-fulfillment.

In broad terms, the dream calls for the impregnation of the young women by an independent masculine spirit, represented by the black man who cuts his own path across uncharted land. This figure compensates the conscious attitude of the dreamer, his fear of what people might say. Collective opinions and lone creative work are opposites; the help of the dreamer's black man, an aspect of himself that is not vulnerable to public opinion, will be required to bring forth the fruits of the unconscious, source of his creative work.

Jung observed that in a man's psychology "the unconscious is often personified by the anima,"[13] which in the imagery of this dream is represented by the two daughters. The anima in turn embodies the principle of Eros.

Apparently the dreamer's Eros wants to maintain its autonomy, not be contaminated by Logos, hence the daughters' reluctance to take the spittle-sperm. This problem could be exacerbated by the dreamer's typology, predominantly introverted feeling. His extraverted thinking would therefore be inferior, prone to be complexed, making him sensitive to collective opinion.

Returning to our myth, Yurlunggur's sibling relationship to the Wawilaks ("Yurlunggur was older brother to these women, and they were sisters to him") underscores the importance of the recurring incest motif; however there is a twist. Jung makes the point that regression is not merely sexually motivated, because ultimately the libido seeks a deeper layer in the unconscious where overt sexual language is replaced by metaphors that involve the procreative, nutritive

---

[13] "Psychology and Religion," *Psychology and Religion: West and East,* CW 11, par. 107.

and digestive functions.[14] This is seen in the myth, where the regressive libido eventually desexualizes itself through rituals mainly concerned with the assurance of the fertility of both the land and humans; this means that the nutritive and digestive elements are sustained by the seasons of plenty that occur each year. In this regard the Murngin relate to the symbolism of the penetration as representing more than the physical act of sex.

What is the symbolic meaning of incest in the myth? To reduce both Yurlunggur's incestuous desire and the sisters' consorting with the Wongar men to nothing but a drive for wish-fulfillment is to deny the life-giving potential in a constructive interpretation. Amplifying the symbolism of such images introduces the possibility for the individual personality to grow beyond its current conflicts. After dreams of homosexual or heterosexual acts, for instance, people are often left ashamed or confused because they assume the Freudian view of the dream as a reflection of a subliminal desire.

While that possibility cannot be dismissed out of hand, on further examination such dreams can frequently be seen as demonstrating a desire to integrate those parts of the dreamer's personality which are represented in the dream by the sexual partner. If it were left to the ego these traits are just as likely to remain buried in the unconscious, and the challenge of becoming a more complete personality would be avoided. This is commented upon by Jung:

> Whenever this drive for wholeness appears, it begins by disguising itself under the symbolism of incest, for, unless he seeks it in himself, a man's nearest feminine counterpart is to be found in his mother, sister, or daughter.[15]

The myth tells us that the Wawilak sisters are frightened and do not want to enter an incestuous union, reflecting the ego attitude appropriate to the collective patriarchal values of the tribe. However, behind the incest taboo is a greater motif than simply the desire to ex-

---

14 *Symbols of Transformation,* CW 5, par. 654.
15 "The Psychology of the Transference," *The Practice of Psychotherapy,* CW 16, par. 471.

pand the network of marriage and social contacts. Ultimately it is concerned with the transformation of instinct into spirit. Up to this point the Wawilaks' involvement with Yurlunggur has been unconscious. Now, in the more conscious sphere, they are faced with the other side of incest; they face symbolic union with a god.

From the viewpoint of personal psychology, the Wawilaks and Yurlunggur can be seen as representing the anima and animus respectively. True to the nature of the anima, associated with the principle of Eros, the Wawilaks had not been interested in the meaning of life; rather they brought the principle of life itself to Yurlunggur when he received their blood. On the other hand, the animus, as Logos, tends to raise questions concerning the meaning of life, as reflected in Yurlunggur's inspiring the Wawilaks to ask about the source of the rain. When they asked this question they were in a state of depression or *nigredo*.

This motif also appears in the fairy tale, "The Blue Light."[16] The light has to be rescued from the well (Yurlunggur's pool) by a young soldier before the king's daughter can be saved from the king (dominant collective values). Here the light represents the ultimate spiritual value which brings with it the meaning of life for the young princess and is the final form of the positive animus. Only by receiving this light can she be freed from the negative animus of her father, the king.

Although the Wawilaks have had sexual relations, by virtue of being unmarried they are still virgins. As John Layard points out, the term "virgin" refers etymologically to any unmarried woman, even a mother, and not to her level of sexual experience.[17] He further suggests that a truer meaning of the word would be "virgin of the soul," describing a woman who has not yet had an active inner relationship with the masculine. Hence the Wawilaks' fear of establishing a conscious relationship with Yurlunggur. They prefer to hide behind the laws of the tribe. However when their camp is penetrated and they

---

16 *The Complete Grimm's Fairy Tales,* no. 116.
17 *The Virgin Archetype,*   p. 289.

are swallowed by the Rainbow Serpent, in effect they are ravished by the god and impregnated by him. At the same time, he is filled with creative potential.

This part of the myth is analogous to the Christian story of the Holy Ghost penetrating the Virgin Mary. Psychologically the feminine principle, represented by the anima-virgin, is joined to the masculine *spiritus mercurialis,* and the dominant attitude of the myth, the mother, is pierced by the phallic masculine. In this way the snake symbolizes the *principium individuonis,* which is the energy intent on serving the growth of consciousness.

In the dream described earlier, where a colored snake swallowed the arm of an aboriginal woman, we can see a parallel to the central motif of our myth. In both the dream and the myth the feminine principle activates the principle of individuation. The dream image compensates the dreamer's ego intent of fulfilling the conventional expectations of society, challenging him to pursue the path of the snake, his individual way. More specifically, the dream indicates that before this essential masculine spirit can be activated, he would have to come to terms with the mystery of the anima. Since the dream came when his interest in life was at a low ebb, it would seem that his projection of the anima outside himself was becoming problematic. Just as the Wawilaks brought Yurlunggur into the consciousness of the tribe, so the work ahead for the dreamer involved the integration of the feminine principle.

Until a man's anima is made conscious, the true masculine spirit remains asleep because she is the psychopomp who will lead him to the inner treasure. As Jung says, "Everything [she] touches becomes numinous—unconditional, dangerous, taboo, magical."[18] Thus the dreamer is challenged to overcome his fear of the unconscious.

Such a path is not without its perils. The dream image suggests the possibility of being completely consumed by the snake, a state in which the ego would be absorbed by the unconscious, that is, a

---

[18] "Archetypes of the Collective Unconscious," *The Archetypes and the Collective Unconscious,* CW 9i, par. 51.

psychosis. This danger is also stressed by the alchemists who warned that "many have perished" in pursuit of the *lapis.*[19]

## The Two As One

Throughout Australia the gender of the Rainbow Serpent varies. In Berndt's version of the Wawilak myth, the snake is unmistakably female even though she produces sperm when she penetrates the camp. The paradox is overcome by Yurlunggur having a snake husband of the same name, thus both masculine and feminine aspects of the snake are clearly embodied.[20] From this it would seem that Yurlunggur has the ability to appear in either guise. In Warner's version he is the great male god, but he also has the quality of a devouring mother, symbolically represented by his ability to swallow people. Hence he has distinctly feminine characteristics, much as the great female goddesses, the Djanggawuls, had a distinct masculine quality (penis-sized clitorises). The Wawilaks as anima figures are the force that link the two worlds.

The Rainbow Serpent's hermaphroditic nature links him with the alchemists' Mercurius duplex, the incarnation of the opposites in one body. Jung observes: "Sometimes his body is said to be masculine and his soul feminine, sometimes the reverse."[21] And so it is in his masculine guise that Mercurius-Yurlunggur appears in Warner's version of the myth. Through the act of swallowing the Wawilaks and their sons he integrates the feminine and masculine aspects of his psyche into a totality. The women and their sons are images of both sides of his unconscious hermaphrodism. By swallowing them he becomes conscious of them as part of himself. No longer will they remain autonomous and hungry for the comfort of the parents, particularly the all-nourishing Great Mother.

---

[19] Turba, Sermon XV (quoted by Jung in "The Visions of Zosimos," *Alchemical Studies,* CW 13, par. 139n.

[20] *Kunapipi,* p. 25.

[21] "The Spirit Mercurius," *Alchemical Studies,* CW 13, par. 268.

However Yurlunggur is still not fully aware of their meaning because he has eaten them whole. Their deeper symbolic value will only become apparent once he has had time to digest and process what they represent. Also, the boys are still minor figures, which indicates that masculine consciousness will continue to be incidental as long as the Yiritja moeity, and particularly their god, Laintjung, has no prominent role to play. For the remainder of the myth they continue to represent merely Yurlunggur's potential masculine maturity.

Significantly there are now four elements contained in Yurlunggur—the two women and the two boys—representing the basic fourfold structure that is held together in a newly created body. Jung refers to Paracelsus' belief that "the physician should see to it that the 'anatomy' (= structure) of the four elements 'be contracted into one anatomy of the microcosm.'"[22] It is a fifth principle, the *quinta essentia,* which contains these four elements; all together they form the principle of the *spiritus mercurius.* There has been a concretization of the psychic elements, a *coagulatio.*[23]

Redemption is mutual: the Wawilaks' instincts are imbued with spirit, and the god receives a soul. The contribution the myth makes to an understanding of the birth of the psyche is to emphasize that the Self figure does not do it by itself; the active participation of all aspects of a person is required. Jung acknowledged this:

[The Self] is the smallest of the small, easily overlooked and pushed aside. Indeed, it is in need of help and must be perceived, protected, and as it were built up by the conscious mind, just as if it did not exist at all and were called into being only through man's care and devotion. . . . The self does not become conscious by itself, but has always been taught, if at all, through a tradition of knowing. . . . It stands for the essence of individuation [which] is impossible without a relationship to one's environment.[24]

---

[22] "Paracelsus as a Spiritual Phenomenon," ibid., par. 171.

[23] See Edward F. Edinger, *Anatomy of the Psyche: Alchemical Symbolism in Psychotherapy,* chapt. 4.

[24] *Aion,* CW 9ii, par. 257.

Thus it requires Yurlunggur to enter into a relationship with the Wawilaks who brought the natural environment into consciousness through naming and cooking. It is through them that Yurlunggur is freed from his prison of unconsciousness and stagnation, just as it is through him that they acknowledge the mysteries of the nonmaterial realm.

After he swallows the women, Yurlunggur is able to become a superior being, of greater stature than the other snakes.

He raised himself and stood very straight. He was like the trunk of a very tall straight tree. His head reached as high as a cloud. When he raised himself to the sky the flood waters came up as he did. They flooded and covered the entire earth. No tree or hill showed above them. When he fell later, the water receded, and at the same time there was dry ground.

Yurlunggur achieved a higher psychological development than the other reptiles as a result of integrating the Eros figures. The others continued to eat only animals and remained stuck in the world of the untransformed libido.

Yurlunggur started cleansing his mouth with his cheeks and tongue. He spat several times. He said to his sons, "I'm going to spew." He regurgitated the two women and the little boys. They were dropped into an ants' nest.

The Wessel Island snake, when he heard what Yurlunggur said, was disgusted. "You've eaten your own wakus and yeppas," he said. This was a terrible thing.

The Wongar Yurlunggur crawled slowly back to his water hole. He went inside but kept his head up to watch. At this time the Yurlunggur trumpet came out of the well and lay beside him. No one brought it out and no one blew it, but it sang out like it does now.

The Yurlunggur trumpet blew over the two women and their two sons. They were lying there like they had fainted. Some green ants came out then and bit the women and children. They jumped.

The trumpet continued to walk around, while the Wongar Yurlunggur looked on. The women and children were alive again, and he had thought them dead. He picked up two singing sticks (bilmel) and crawled out of the water hole.

In this part of the myth Yurlunggur vomits up the Wawilaks unconscious or dead; however, through no actions of his own, they are
revitalized. First the didgeridoo or trumpet magically blows over
them; that is, they receive the breath of the transmundane god, a
mysterious integrative force, perhaps called into being through the
relationship between the snake and the sisters.

Here we see a link being made between the breath of god and the
energy inherent in the feminine principle. There is a parallel to this
phenomenon in the Judeo-Christian tradition where the Wisdom of
God was also feminine: "She is the breath of the power of God."[25]
It is as if through this action the women formally become the anima
of Yurlunggur. "Anima" in Latin means "something breathing" or
"blowing";[26] Jung described the anima as "the archetype of life itself";[27] and so the sisters become Yurlunggur's breath of life.

A transformation of this kind can only happen when one has un-
dergone a night sea journey, a dark night of the soul, akin to the
Wawilaks' experience inside the snake's body. Through receiving
the breath one's physical and psychic realms become firmly united.
Like Mercurius, Yurlunggur is essentially an archetypal image of
unity. The analogy in alchemy is the production of the *corpus sub-
tile*,[28] the transfigured and resurrected body. Something similar occurs in the analytic process where contents of the unconscious are
brought to light and transformed only through the mysterious intervention of the Self—or as Jung often says, *Deo concedente*—and not
through will power. So too, the transformation of Yurlunggur could
only occur through divine grace.

The other aspect to the Wawilaks' revivification is their being bitten by green ants. A bite from a green ant results in symptoms not
dissimilar to those of a fever; the heart beats faster, the sweat glands

---

[25] Wisdom of Solomon 7:25, Authorized Version.

[26] *Cassels Latin Dictionary.*

[27] "Archetypes of the Collective Unconscious," *The Archetypes and the
Collective Unconscious*, CW 9i, par. 66.

[28] *Psychology and Alchemy*, CW 12, par. 511.

secrete more abundantly and one is altogether very uncomfortable. Presumably the Wawilaks experience such symptoms, akin to sensations that arise when the sympathetic nervous system is stimulated. Indeed, the ants can be seen as symbolizing this part of the anatomy. Through their contact with the ants, the Wawilaks acquire the capacity to respond to the range of feelings that stimulate the sympathetic nervous system, including pain, fear, love and any other strong emotion. Thus the ants represent the capacity to respond in a feeling way. Ultimately it will be through them that this capacity will be passed on to Yurlunggur when he reswallows them.

A similar motif appeared in the dream of a man who strongly identified with a pure persona, in much the same way as the Wawilak sisters ("We are good, and we are clean.") He dreamed he was in a room standing on a glass floor which covered a sea of ants, relieved that they could not get to him.

This man's attitude to the outside world was influenced by his mother complex, reflected in the claim that he liked his soft and sentimental "feminine" side. (Jung: "An infantile man generally has a maternal anima.")[29] Not surprisingly, he had a brutal shadow side that unconsciously ran his life. Because his feelings stemmed from his mother complex rather than his own nature, he was unable to develop lasting relationships with women. Eventually he always felt suffocated by the projection of mother onto his partners. The glass floor in the dream shows that he is insulated from his own spontaneous feelings. It could also suggest that he had only an intellectual appreciation of his problems.

Before being bitten by the ants, the Wawilak women had been in a position inferior to that of Yurlunggur. They were easily terrorized by him. (On a personal level, this would be equivalent to a dominant and one-sided masculine attitude, to the point where the feminine is overwhelmed.) Now there is a complete reversal. Through the Wawilaks Yurlunggur gets into touch with a central aspect of the

---

[29] "The Psychological Aspects of the Kore," *The Archetypes and the Collective Unconscious,* CW 9i, par. 357.

feminine, namely relatedness—with respect to both other individuals and one's own sources of creativity.

After they have been revived the Wawilaks are swallowed again.

> He hit the mothers and their babies on their heads with the sticks and swallowed them again. He meant to keep them down this time.
>
> He felt sick again, for once more he had swallowed Dua people. He decided to stand up straight.
>
> When he raised up the mandelpui snake shouted, "What did you eat?"
>
> "Bandicoot," he lied.
>
> "You do not tell the truth."
>
> "The two Dua women and the two Yiritja boys."
>
> When he said this he fell again. This time he made the Gunabibi and Ulmark dance grounds by his fall (as the first time he fell he formed a Djungguan place). After his fall, he crawled into the Liaalaomir well and went down into the subterranean waters.

We are left with an image of the unconscious that Jung has described as "the spirit of chthonic nature [which] contains the archetypal images of the *Sapientia Dei.* "[30] This image of mutual dependence of the feminine and masculine aspects in the god figure is also similar to one that Gilles Quispel has observed where "Christ needs Sophia and Sophia needs Christ."[31] The Wawilaks' containment in the Rainbow Serpent is the ultimate *coniunctio* where the opposites come together, with Yurlunggur representing the masculine, water and air, and the Wawilaks the feminine, earth and fire. The meaning of this integration of the opposites is conveyed in a saying of Jesus:

> When you make the two into one
> And what is within like what is without . . .
> And when you unite male and female in one
> So that the male is no longer male,
> And the female no longer female . . .
> Then you shall enter the Kingdom.[32]

---

[30] "The Psychology of the Transference," *The Practice of Psychotherapy,* CW 16, par. 480.

[31] "Gnosis and the New Sayings of Jesus," *Eranos Jahrbuch,* 1969, p. 289.

[32] *The Gospel According to Thomas,* logion 22, p. 24.

With the opposites united in one body, the fertility of both the land and themselves is assured. This union is the focus of the Gunabibi and Ulmark rituals. The end result is similar to the vision of Arisleus where the land was unfruitful because the practice of exogamous incest prevailed (like was only mating with like). In this vision, the alchemist advised the king to join his son with his daughter and "make the land fruitful again by means of a brother-sister incest."[33] In other words the advice was to unite the opposite tendencies in a conscious manner. At a collective level, this union is seen in the form of the wet season (Yurlunggur), and the dry (the Wawilaks being from the land) being brought together because, for the productive dry period to occur, there must be a wet season to fertilize the land.

On a personal level among the Murngin, the *coniunctio* involves the initiation of young men, which takes place during the Gunabibi ceremony. Here the rituals symbolize the process through which the individual is transformed in much the same way that Yurlunggur was. That the legend of Yurlunggur should provide a model for the boys' transformation is psychologically right because otherwise it would occur only at the behest of the ego. It would be a creation of the will rather than a command from the unconscious. Jung writes: "It is . . . the god who transforms himself, and only through him does man take part in the transformation."[34]

To become a man the youth is smeared with the blood of the Wawilaks and told to go out into the bush. The significance of the blood is that, through it, the initiate symbolically becomes a woman, to be sought and swallowed by the snake. Psychologically, this means that he is enabled to experience the anima, the feminine side of his personality. An uninitiated boy has no real sexual identity. The first identity he receives is that of a woman. He symbolically goes through the same experiences the Wawilaks had, and ultimately it will be the aspect of his psyche represented by them that will animate the dormant snake. In other words, he can only enter a man's world

---

[33] *Psychology and Alchemy,* CW 12, par. 496.
[34] *Symbols of Transformation,* CW 5, par. 389.

after he has been a woman, experiencing the instinctual drives of nature and transforming them. Then he can be inducted into the male domain of tribal secrets.

The dream referred to earlier with the colored snake ends where the aboriginal woman presents the dreamer with a tie made from snake skin (page 32). It has been noted that the dreamer's energy was largely extraverted and that the anima had been devalued and therefore somewhat unconscious. For most of the dreamer's life this had not been a problem. As Jung observed about younger men, they "can bear even the total loss of the anima without injury. . . . The growing youth must be able to free himself from the anima fascination of his mother."[35] After mid life, however, living without a conscious relationship to the anima becomes a problem. And just so, this dreamer could no longer tolerate a life without zest. (Jung: "Permanent loss of the anima means a diminution of vitality.")[36]

When the anima figure presents the dreamer with a snake tie he is symbolically led toward initiation into the world of the masculine spirit. He must accept and trust her as psychopomp. By wearing the tie he has the symbol of a snake coiled around his neck, connecting head and body, just as Yurlunggur coiled around the Wawilaks' camp. Should he betray the python spirit he would run the risk of incurring its wrath. It might contract and threaten his life. The tie is therefore a constant reminder of the cost of living an unbalanced life.

In some aboriginal tribes there is a ceremony of subincision where a cut is made along the youth's penis to represent a vagina, a living symbol of the receptive feminine. The initiate will then be called upon to reenact this process during later ceremonies when he will give his blood for the initiation of other novices. The blood will come either from the "vagina" of the penis or from an opening in his forearm. In this way, throughout his life, he ritually reexperiences his feminine side.

---

[35] "Concerning the Archetypes and the Anima Concept," *The Archetypes and the Collective Unconscious,* CW 9i, par. 146.
[36] Ibid., par. 147.

An aboriginal novice being bathed in his sponsor's blood, to initiate
him into the society of men.
(From Francis Huxley, *The Way of the Sacred*)

Again the age-grading ceremony is a description of the individuation process; however, just as it was with Yurlunggur, the initiation is one-sided because it takes place only within Mother Nature. The secrets the initiate receives are those concerned with her because the whole of the society is derived from nature. The emphasis is on the collective and excludes any celebration of the individual. With masculine symbols such as Laintjung, the Wawilak boys and the snake itself either excluded or insignificant, there is no opposite tendency present. Thus the society will remain identified with a collective attitude.

As Jung observed, as long as there is no sense of inner contradiction, the individual psyche will remain primitive, that is, collective.[37]

In the final scene Yurlunggur takes the Wawilaks back to their own country.

> He put a stone over his entrance and stopped the flood of water that had been coming out. He swam in the underground waters to the Wawilak country, for he wanted to take the mothers and children back to their own country; here he spat them out for the last time. He left them there and came back to his own country. The two women turned to stone and one can still see them in the Wawilak country today. Yurlunggur kept the boys inside him, for they were Yiritja and he was Dua.

Stopping the flow of water from the well represents an arrest in the flow of energy that had been streaming out of the unconscious; Yurlunggur thereby allows a greater state of consciousness to prevail. This is reinforced when he deposits the Wawilaks on the surface of the land, the conscious realm. There they turn into the stones which can be seen today and represent the sisters' totem. Thus Yurlunggur inducts them into the daily spiritual life of the Murngin. But for him they would have disappeared; in effect, the Wawilaks would be dead to the consciousness of the Murngin and also it would be impossible to make a link with Yurlunggur.

---

[37] "The Relations Between the Ego and the Unconscious," *Two Essays on Analytical Psychology,* CW 7, par. 237.

Through these actions Yurlunggur, in his wisdom, decided that the value of the Wawilaks would first have to be recognized before he could be activated. Psychologically this means that the individual has to experience and integrate the anima before the masculine spirit can be aroused.

Significantly, Yurlunggur himself is not represented as a natural feature in the spiritual life of the Murngin; it is simply assumed that he lives at the bottom of the well. The only time he is manifested in physical form is during the Gunabibi rituals as a *jelmalandji* pole, the making of which represents energy consciously directed toward Yurlunggur.[38] However the pole can only be used after the Wawilaks have made the link to him. The anima-Wawilaks are therefore the connection between the two worlds, a "bridge to the unconscious . . . a function of relationship to the unconscious."[39] In keeping with their role as psychopomps, they pass on the mysteries of the rituals to two men via a dream:

> They [the two men] slept, and while they were in a deep sleep they dreamed of what the two women sang and danced when they were trying to keep Yurlunggur from swallowing them. The Wawilak women came back as spiritis and taught the two men the Djungguan songs and dances . . . . They told the men the way to do the Marndiella, Gunabibi, and Ulmark ceremonies. . . .
>
> The two sisters said to men, "This is all now. We are giving you this dream so you can remember these important things. You must never forget these things we have told you tonight."

At the end of the myth the boys stay with Yurlunggur in his underground world, representing the masculine principle deeply buried in the psyche of the Murngin. It will be the task of the medicine-man to bring the masculine to consciousness and to establish an individual relationship with contents of the unconscious. This process will be described in chapter four.

---

[38] See below, p. 56.

[39] Jung, "Commentary on *The Secret of the Golden Flower*," *Alchemical Studies,* CW 13, par. 62.

# 3
# The Failed Masculine

By the end of the myth, the Wawilak rituals have been established. Yurlunggur, with the boys inside him (his masculine potential) presumably returned to the Mirrirmina well, sealed off from the rest of the world. Everything he represented disappears from consciousness. In a similar manner the Murngin leave no outer evidence of the Wawilak rituals; they bury, hide and even destroy their sacred objects after the ceremonies have been completed. It seems that the deep meaning of the myth is relegated to and kept in the unconscious part of the aboriginal psyche—with Yurlunggur.

The prevailing sense of unconsciousness that surrounds the myth is reinforced through its ritualization being conveyed to two men through a dream. This is reflected by the participants when they enter the ceremonies in a state of *participation mystique* with nature and mythical beings. No differentiation is made between the inner and outer worlds, nor between subject and object. Although this brings the participants into a relationship with the unconscious, there is no conscious awareness of the meaning behind the ceremonies.

Even such a limited experience can be healing, of course, particularly for Western individuals in that it at least they become aware of the existence of the unconscious. But the Aborigine in *participation mystique* with the environment becomes a living part of Mother Nature. Add to this the fact that the ceremonies are owned by the feminine Dua moiety and we can conclude that there is an overwhelming predominance of the feminine at the expense of the masculine.

Being at one with Mother Nature has its price. A strong identification with any archetype precludes the possibility of a conscious relationship with it. As long as there is a weak boundary between an archetypal image and the ego, a collective life is inevitable. Individual self-expression is precluded and genuine relationships are not possible. The man who identifies with the archetype of the mother, for instance, is unable to see a woman's individual qualities; he has no discriminating masculine viewpoint. The same is true of a woman in thrall to the father archetype; she cannot see a man as he is.

The effects of the lack of a conscious masculine presence is the subject of this chapter.

## Lu'ningu and Lumaluma

In the Djanggawul myth recorded by Berndt, referred to in chapter one, there is a male figure, Laintjung, responsible for establishing the masculine Yiritja moeity and its associated rituals. Like the Djanggawuls, he came from the sea; he represents the masculine counterpoint to the Djanggawul sisters.

> The Djanggawul, on arrival at Port Bradshaw, were thrown into immediate association with the *jiritja* [Yiritja] Beings, Laintjung and the Baijini [the pre-Macassan people]. Laintjung is the *jiritja* male counterpart of the Djanggawul; he, with his son Banaitja, and certain associated females, is often said to have been responsible for bringing into being the ancestors of the *jiritja* moiety people. . . . Laintjung, then, is legitimately contemporaneous with the Djanggawul.[1]

When Laintjung died, his son Banaitja decided to put his father's religious concepts into practice, which meant that a direct challenge was made to the traditional Dua rituals. His efforts aroused the antagonism of the Dua men and he was driven out and killed. We know that these Dua actions were effective because of the secondary role played by Yiritja rituals. The victory over Banaitja resulted in the Yiritja moeity remaining inferior to the Dua; to this day its members assist in the Dua ceremonies but are not entrusted with any of the deep secrets; that is, the masculine principle is suppressed by the feminine.

---

[1] Berndt, *Djanggawul*, p. 54.

The result of all this is that one aspect of the aboriginal psyche is excluded. The feminine principle (Eros, nature) prevails, while the masculine (discriminating Logos) remains unconscious. As long as there is no opposite attitude to consider, there is no inner contradiction, no conflict, and the tribal mentality will stay the same. (Jung: "There is no consciousness without discrimination of opposites.")[2] Past practices will continue because there is no viewpoint from which to question them; a collective rather than an individual attitude will prevail.

Dua conservatism functions like a protective mother. The Great Mother does not voluntarily give up her secrets, rather she demands the right attitude from those entering her domain if she is to share her mysteries. The challenge is to understand the language and images of her message. The deepest revelations are made through myth. *"God always speaks mythologically,"* writes Jung. "If he didn't, he would reveal reason and science."[3] It requires a well-directed conscious attitude to discover the secrets of the Dua-unconscious, and the Yiritja proved not to have this ability.

On the one hand, Banaitja represents a potential consciousness in that he wanted to teach his religious practices. On the other, the Yiritja moiety represents a masculine principle which lacked sufficient power to enter into an active relationship with its dominant feminine counterpart.

In Berndt's version of the myth a figure similar to that of Banaitja is introduced. This is Lu'ningu, an unmarried male python that came out of the Mirrirmina well where he saw Yurlunggur swallow and then regurgitate the Wawilaks.[4] The fact that he resided next to Yurlunggur in the well suggests that he is Yurlunggur's brother and represents the shadow side of the great snake.

When Lu'ningu saw Yurlunggur vomit up the Wawilaks he

---

[2] "Psychological Aspects of the Mother Archetype," *The Archetypes and the Collective Unconscious,* CW 9i, par. 178.

[3] *C.G. Jung Letters,* vol. 2, p. 9 (italics in original).

[4] *Kunapipi,* p. 35.

thought he could do the same and went around the countryside swallowing all the unmarried boys. However when he regurgitated the boys they were all dead and would not revive. Their flesh had been removed and only their skeletons remained.

Through this action Lu'ningu demonstrated that he had no individuality of his own. By merely aping what he saw, Lu'ningu was blind to his responsibility to understand its significance. But his greatest crime was that he was Yiritja and this represented a masculine invasion into exclusive feminine territory, posing a potential threat to the stable social order of the tribe. In response, the men decided that he should be eliminated, so they hunted him and speared him to death. Effectively, he had colluded with the Dua because, by imitating their god instead of establishing his own standpoint, he perpetuated their dominance. As Jung has observed about the faculty of imitation, it is "the most pernicious for individuation" and "the greatest utility for collective purposes."[5] Clearly this applies equally to any culture.

In the rituals as reported by Berndt, there is a scene where two *jelmalandji* poles are erected.

> They compared Lu'ningu with Julunggul [Yurlunggur], saying: "Lu'ningu is no good, he vomits up his people dead. But Julunggul is all right; he vomited up the Wauwalak so that they were alive." So they hunted out Lu'ningu , spearing him until he died.
>
> "What are we going to do?" they asked one another then. So they made a large *jelmalandji* which stood upright in the ground, in memory of this snake. . . . They built another *jelmalandji*, larger than the first, to represent the Julunggul who swallowed the Wauwalak.[6]

In addition to the two poles which are usually about twenty feet high, a third pole is laid on the ground. Then the two upright poles are repeatedly pushed over so that they crash onto the third pole. Since all this occurs when contact is made between Yurlunggur and

---

[5] "The Relations Between the Ego and the Unconscious," *Two Essays on Analytical Psychology*, CW 7, par. 242.

[6] *Kunapipi*, pp. 35-36.

the Wawilaks, one can speculate that this part of the ritual shows the opposites being bridged by the third, the transcendent function. They are symbolically brought into union.

The question remains as to who is represented by the two poles, and what pair of opposites is brought into union. In the above passage, undoubtedly one of them is Julunggul-Yurlunggur, who in Berndt's version is female, and the other is Lu'ningu, who is male. However elsewhere in Berndt's account the identity of the snake represented by the smaller pole is not always clear.

At one point, for example, it appears that the smaller pole is the husband of Julunggul, while at another it is the masculine spirit of Julunggul.[7] The only common element is that this pole represents a masculine principle. The uncertainty surrounding the masculine pole suggests that this aspect is much less differentiated than was the feminine. On this reading the knocking down of the two poles onto the third would represent the union between the masculine and feminine aspects of Yurlunggur at the level of the earth, the level of consciousness. However there are further complications.

Significantly, the two poles are pushed down until the "other" is broken, that is, until the pandanus leaves are knocked off the smaller "masculine" pole. This means that the ritual process results in the clearly defined or pure masculine aspect being broken off. It is driven out of the potential consciousness of the tribe, with the result that this central myth highlights only the feminine aspects of the tribe. This creates the paradoxical situation whereby the feminine principle is integrated but the masculine is rejected. In other words the Wawilaks, who initially represent Eros, relatedness, are brought into union with Yurlunggur, or Logos, but Lu'ningu, his phallic aspect, is driven off. Psychologically this means that the masculine is split off from the psyche and becomes an autonomous complex.

These dynamics are relevant to the case of an analysand who had long suffered from severe somatic problems. He also had become aware that he had no ego identity of his own, that it had been ab-

---

[7] Ibid., p. 38.

sorbed by his father. In place of a personal masculine standpoint was a collective one, a highly refined and cultivated spiritual attitude which dominated his life. It was split off and had become an autonomous complex that colored much of his character.

This man did not know of my interest in aboriginal mythology nor was he aware of any aboriginal myths. On the very night that I was working on the meaning behind this part of the myth he had the following dream.

> I was a student in a high school. I left to go home but along the way I met a native woman whom I had earlier told I would like to climb a glass mountain. She did not encourage me. Then I was lowered into a circular pit which had feathers, stones and a loin cloth associated with it. I emerged from the pit and felt initiated. Later I reached my home which was opposite the big glass mountain.

The dreamer's associations to the high school were that it represented an oppressive patriarchy he had to get away from. The implication is that he has to leave the father complex behind before he can deal with the grandiose world of the spirit (the glass mountain). The anima does not encourage him to climb the mountain. An alternative is presented. He finds himself lowered into a hole, suggesting that his task is to come down from the elevated spiritual world to the underground, the chthonic realm.

In part of the aboriginal initiation ceremony involving the feathered *jelmalandji* poles, a circular hole or *nanggaru* is dug, which the boys are made to enter. They symbolically enter the mother, an interpretation reinforced by one of the aboriginal associations with the *nanggaru* as a vagina. All this is done before the boys are ceremonially eaten by the snake and admitted to the spiritual world.

These motifs are relevant to the above dreamer, who had a poor relation to the earth (hence a number of floating dreams) and, more particularly, to his own body. The dream picks up his need to become more grounded and immerse himself in earthy matters. The image of the loin cloth next to the hole suggests that entering the realm of the feminine goes hand in hand with his masculine development.

In other words the dream, and particularly the native anima figure, directs him to relate more consciously to the feminine.

The masculine quality that the Murngin are so intent to suppress, be it in the form of Banaitja or Lu'ningu, manifests in the figure of Lumaluma who combines the features of both.

Although Lumaluma is from neither of the two tribes witnessed by Warner and Berndt, he is a mythical being who belongs to a tribe immediately to the south and the area in which the myth originated. He was a religious figure who not only had his own rituals and beliefs but, like Lu'ningu and Banaitja, also wanted to be a religious leader. Because of his ambition to impose his practices on the prevailing Dua moeity he was speared to death, as Banaitja was, and now lives as a whale, while Banaitja lives as a barramundi (a large fresh-water fish).

Just as there is the Leviathan in Judeo-Christian tradition, here we meet a similar creature in aboriginal culture. In both traditions this aspect of the godhead resides in the deep waters of the unconscious because, as was to be experienced by both Jonah and the Aborigines, the prevailing collective religious attitude imprisoned it there. For both Jonah and the Aborigines this Leviathan-whale represents the devil, counterbalance to the religious belief that is most palatable to the collective.

With the coming of the white man, the Aborigine would reexperience this nonintegrated psychic component with disastrous consequences, devastating his traditional religious system and way of life. Jonah experienced the inhuman Leviathan quality of Yahweh, just as the Aborigines would experience the inhuman aspect of their male god which they had denied at every opportunity in order to protect the prevailing religion.

## An Archetype of Structure

Another aspect of Lumaluma closely associates him with Lu'ningu because both ate children and regurgitated them until only their skeletons remained. In other words their creativity produced lifeless bones. Presumably this is what would have happened had Lumaluma won the day and his system been introduced.

The picture opposite shows Lumaluma after he was killed. It gives an insight into the psychological dynamics of the motif that would reemerge and have such a dramatic effect on modern day Aborigines. Here we see the forces that are involved when a masculine attitude as symbolized by Lumaluma is constellated.

There are five figures in the picture: Lumaluma, clearly the center, two flying foxes at the top, and the emu and the skeleton of a young boy whom Lumaluma has killed at the bottom. The fact that these four figures are outside the frame of his body and detached from it lends support to the hypothesis that he identifies more with outer events and that these symbolize his conscious reality. At the same time they also reflect inner aspects of himself that have not been integrated. As long as this psychological state is projected onto outer events, his life will be identified with them and he will reflect a collective attitude.

Lumaluma is depicted as a skeleton. The use of an x-ray technique is fairly typical of aboriginal art, where the central subject is usually richly represented by abstracted totemic lines in addition to other figures such as a child, animal or plant. On page 63 is a picture of the Fertility Mother, Waramurunggundji, who is represented in a close relationship with a child and lily roots, showing how the inclusion of sacred lines within a figure give it an internal richness.

This richness suggests that the Aborigines are psychologically close to her inner nature and the symbolic value of her inner life. In addition she has a close connection with children and plants, indicating that they are an integrated part of her psyche and that she is in contact with her intrinsic potential. By contrast, Lumaluma is seen as a skeleton, suggesting that his inner nature has no substance, and his symbolic meaning has yet to be realized.

Lumaluma's imposing figure primarily symbolizes structure. This is exactly what he produces in the spontaneous moment when he vomits up the boys as skeletons. In this instance the essence of his

Bark Painting of Lumaluma.
(From R.M. Berndt, "Images of God in Aboriginal Australia")

creativity is death. As long as such an attitude is dominant, his masculine potential will remain lifeless, devoid of flesh and blood. In this form, Lumaluma-Lu'ningu represents a one-sided Logos principle completely out of touch with the other pole, Eros. It is Logos that was driven off by the Murngin, becoming unconscious to them.

The two flying foxes are the only flying figures we have met so far. For the Murngin the symbol of the flying fox is consciously used to trick the women so that the male domain will not be threatened. For example there is one part to the Gunabibi ceremony where all members of the tribe witness the boys being placed under a mat (symbolizing the hut) to await Yurlunggur's penetration. However rather than sing the phrase that the Wawilaks actually sang before Yurlunggur entered the hut (kei'wa kei'wa), the men sing the song of the flying fox (wa' wa'). Should they sing "kei wa," one of their secrets would become known to the women present, and the men's fear is that the women would then take over the ceremony.

Symbolically this is what the Murngin refer to as the "flying fox side" and it is this side that is in the ascendancy in the picture. Add to this that they are on either side of his head and the meaning of the flying fox side becomes clearer; while they are in this position, there will be no conflict since two identical forces produce no tension. The "other" is not present. He will hear only a common voice from both sides, and the head will have no conflict to mediate. The result is that a male attitude, or Logos, will dominate consciousness.

As mentioned above, the Murngin men use the flying fox side to protect their domain and exclude the women. From this it can be seen that where there is a prevailing male attitude the flying fox becomes important because he symbolizes male dominance. Since the picture shows that Lumaluma has an active relationship with the flying foxes, he represents the protection of the domain of the men and the repression of any feminine presence.

This is further amplified in the picture by the figures below him. In this context, "below" is where the elements that have been consigned to the unconscious will be found. It is the realm opposite to "flying fox" consciousness. Generally in aboriginal mythology the

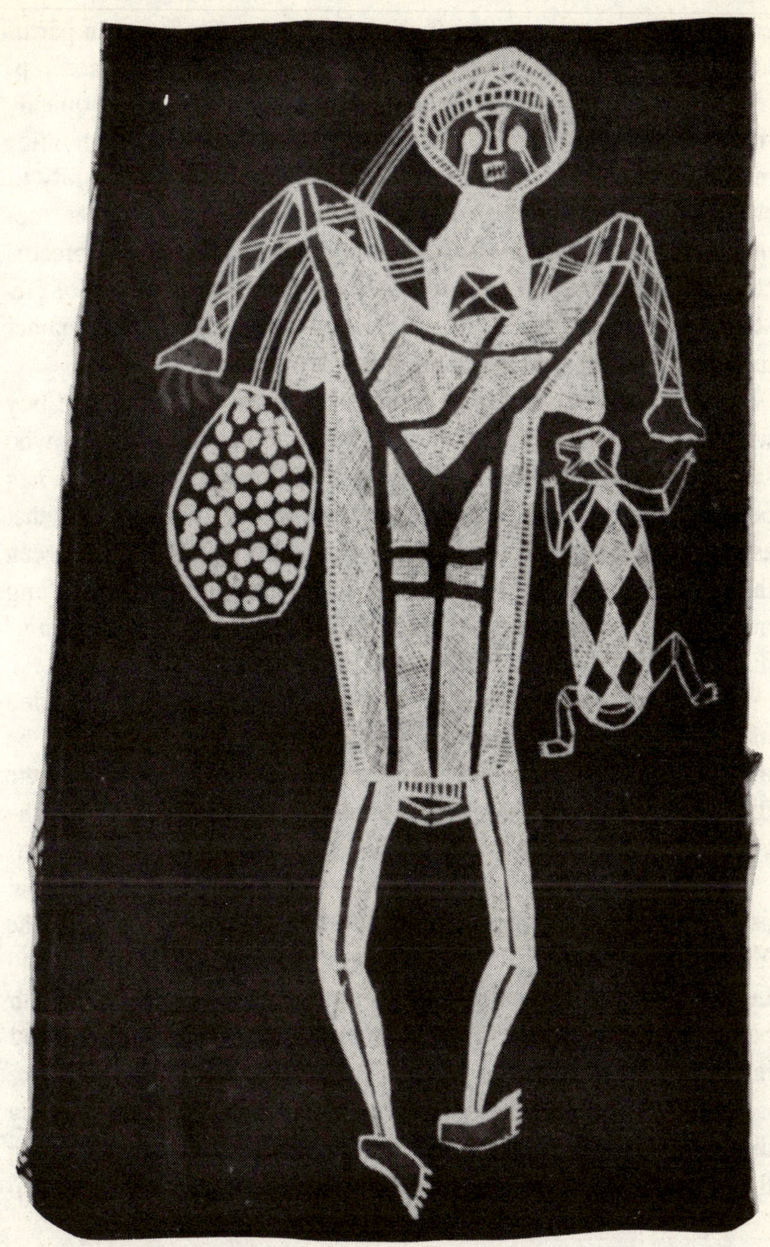

Bark painting of Waramurunggundji, Fertility Mother.
(From R.M. Berndt, "Australian Aboriginal Religion")

emu, with her large eggs, symbolizes a feminine figure and in particular the Great Mother.[9] Because of her speed she has also been represented in mythology as a highly mobile figure able to move quickly from one point to another while along the way collecting anything that attracts her.[10] In this guise she is the antithesis of conformity to established patterns and structures. Rather she responds to the moment, spontaneously, investigating her environment with no preconceived pattern. Looked at in this way the emu is the essence of creativity in that she makes the most out of the specific instance rather than deploying an established approach to a situation.

Confined to the same unconscious realm as the emu is the boy who has been killed by Lumaluma. The paradox is that the boy who symbolizes the potential masculine part of Lumaluma's psyche has been killed by a predominant patriarchal attitude. This is to say that as long as the flying fox is in the ascendant a relationship between the boy and the emu cannot be made conscious, nor can the young masculine be nurtured and brought to maturity by the positive feminine figure. The result is that the potential is starved to death. As long as Lumaluma is in the grip of a flying fox complex, a one-sided male attitude will predominate, his true masculine potential will be thwarted, and he will remain merely an instrument through which the flying fox can exercise its power. Under its regime the emu and the young boy will be unable to contribute to Lumaluma's development.

The Wawilak myth reflects the split that exists in the aboriginal psyche—acceptance of the Dua-feminine side and rejection of the Yiritja-masculine. It is as if Yurlunggur married the feminine and Lu'ningu-Lumaluma married the masculine. In this sense the myth portrays the shadow sides to each moeity, a relationship summarized in the diagram opposite.

The myth is about choice and the Murngin made a clear one by driving Lu'ningu as far out of their psyche as possible, designing their social and religious system around Yurlunggur and the Wawi-

---

[9] L.R. Hiatt, ed., *Australian Aboriginal Mythology,* pp. 34-35.
[10] Ibid.

laks. They saw the opposite principles as representing one or the other, not one *and* the other, and as long as their dilemma is solved in such a manner one side will remain completely unconscious.

Had Yurlunggur somehow been able to integrate the Wawilaks and his shadow brother Lumaluma-Lu'ningu, most likely he would not have returned to the womb of Mother Earth. Rather he would have directed his energies to outer tasks in a classic male fashion and remained on the surface for all to experience, thus becoming part of the conscious world. This did not happen, so it would be the medicine-man who would stand in the middle of the cross, hold the tension between the two attitudes and reconcile them. By doing this he would become a man of "high degree."[10]

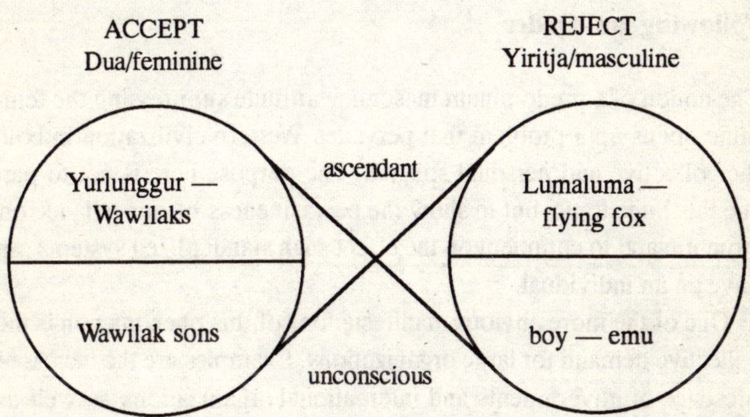


It has already been mentioned that apart from epitomizing the male principle Lumaluma also represents structure. As a skeleton, he represents an attitude devoid of life, his individual masculine potential dead and unable to enter a relationship with the feminine principle, the emu. With all the efforts by the Aborigines to reject and suppress such a figure over the thousands of years of living on the continent, it is not surprising that he would spring into consciousness from an

---

[10] A term coined by Elkin for the medicine-man. See A. P. Elkin, *Aboriginal Men of High Degree*.

unknown place and take over; such is the nature of an autonomous complex. For the Aborigine and the prevailing spirit of the land, the complex or curse that overwhelmed the country was the white man, and Lumaluma can be seen as the archetype of the male attitude that was embraced by white Australia.

The white man and the psychology he represents became the Leviathan or devil that emerged from the deep. The Aborigine was helpless to defend against the onslaught because he had continuously suppressed these forces. The dark shadow of the Aborigine had arrived and would prove to be the antithesis to the irrational world, the living spirit of the land. Nature and the prevailing culture would be disunited and the country would be split.

## Following an Order

The notion of a predominant masculine attitude suppressing the feminine opens up a problem that pervades Western civilization in both the collective and personal spheres. The purpose here is not to pursue this huge topic, but to show the pervasiveness of our reliance on structure and to comment on the effect such standardized systems can have on an individual.

One of the more obvious manifestations of this phenomenon is the collective demand for large organizations. Examples are the increased presence of governments and international organizations as well as the dominant economic role played by multinational companies. At the turn of the century in Australia, one worker in fifty was employed by government whereas today one is three is in its service. A similar pattern is apparent in industry, where in the early 1900s some ten per cent of the manufacturing workforce was employed in firms of twenty or more people; today that figure is approximately eighty per cent.[12]

The need to operate within a structural framework can be seen at the individual level as well. The predilection for such structures can

---

[12] *Australian Year Book,* 1987, pp. 302, 664.

be seen in the general tendency to comply to the traditions that have been handed down through generations. The difficulty of breaking out of such structures is played out daily in the analytic process. Libido gets caught in family patterns and other complexes, whose lure is that they are a more comfortable place from which to operate than an individual but solitary standpoint.

Perhaps these collective and personal trends can best be symbolized by the fact that we are living in the "Computer Age." The design of a computer is very simple in that it is based on the binary number system. No matter how sophisticated it is, the operation of a computer is decided by processing questions which can only be answered by "Yes" or "No." There is no place for a third. The decisions are the simplest possible, black or white—Yurlunggur or Lumaluma. This works well in situations that can be decided on the basis of one *or* the other rather than one *and* the other. Such an approach is in complete contradiction to the process of analytical psychology, and particularly the art of dream interpretation, which is not about "this *or* that" but "this *and* that."[13]

On both a collective and personal level we have a strong tendency to rely on and dutifully serve established structures. The following dreams are presented to illustrate the effect such phenomena can have on a person's creativity and independence.

A man who in real life was a government employee dreamed he was standing before a group of people in the large government department where he worked. He told them about the devastating effect bureaucracy can have on an individual, and pointed out that as long as a person is part of the system it is impossible to be creative. He also mentioned the problem of being caught in various forms of bureaucratic structures without being aware of the fact. The problem was deeply embedded in our society, he said, and even judges were part of it. The dream audience understood what he was saying,

---

13 Jung: "When we think of the unconscious we must think paradoxically, often in terms of yea and nay. . . . That is a very important principle in the interpretation of dreams." (*Dream Analysis: Notes of the Seminar Given in 1928-1930,* p. 132.)

agreed wholeheartedly and was very grateful.

The main meaning of the dream is self-evident, a statement from the unconscious on the effect of the imposition of structures. On a subjective level the bureaucratic structure is comprised of those inner figures and voices to whom we have to report and from whom we must receive approval before we can express ourselves. If they are part of a worn-out tradition of parental views or community standards, we will be unable to express ourselves in an individual manner and remain merely dutiful members of the tribe. The dream states that as long as we are working for a bureaucracy, either external or internal, the effect on our creativity is negative. In particular it singles out judges, who both represent and impose traditional community standards.

It is the role of a judge to assess the seriousness of a crime and in this context he represents an evaluating principle. Of the four functions postulated by Jung, evaluation is related to the feeling function. From the dream, then, the added comment is that this function is caught up in collective structures and hence, as long as such organizations prevail and our dependence on them continues, feelings will merely reflect collective values and there will be an absence of individual expression. It would seem that the message of the dream is understood since it is enthusiastically received by those who have been most affected by such an organization.

There is a second dream which suggests a solution to the problems concerning structure. The dreamer was hovering just above the ground in the company of a number of government employees. Gradually he began to float down until he was under the ground. He came to rest in a large crucible where he felt the relief of being completely solitary. He then realized he was not alone and that a young boy, small and frail, was in the crucible with him.

Coming down to earth and ending up in a container is a motif we met in a dream referred to earlier (page 58), where the dreamer ended up in a pit. There is also a parallel to the symbolism in the picture of Lumaluma. In the dream the governing principle is the floating effect, which shows that the flying fox side is active in the ivory towers of modern government. It is this that would keep the individual in the world of bureaucratic order, or Lumaluma's structure, established to serve the needs of the collective. Such needs are consolidated in the power of the politician. As Jung observed, so long as collective qualities are demanded of individuals, a premium will be placed on mediocrity. "Individuality will eventually be driven to the wall."[14]

It is the flying fox that would keep the dreamer identified with collective structures. The movement in the dream takes him out of the bureaucratic structure where he is floating, not grounded, and brings him to a reality that is below, a world suppressed by the spirit of Lumaluma. This is where the dreamer will be able to relate to his own masculine potential. The relationship will develop in the crucible which, in this context, would symbolize the nurturing mother. It is also in the crucible or "uterus" that the process of transformation takes place, from a collective to an individual identity.[15]

The young boy in the dream symbolizes the basic potential for the synthesis of the personality. According to Jung, the child is "something that is always becoming, is never completed, and calls for unceasing care, attention and education. That is the part of the human personality which wants to develop and become whole."[16]

In the dream the boy is analogous to the alchemical homunculus or *lapis philosophorum,* "smaller than small," the spirit of Mercurius. This figure is related to the multicolored peacock, the *cauda pavonis,* archetypally equivalent to the Rainbow Serpent.

There is also a remarkable parallel between this dream, the Lumaluma figure, and a vision of Zosimos related by Jung. In this vision Zosimos saw a priest standing before an altar in the shape of a shallow bowl.[17] The priest descended into the darkness and revealed

---

[14] "The Relations Between the Ego and the Unconscious," *Two Essays on Analytical Psychology,* CW 7, par. 240.

[15] See above, p. 22.

[16] "The Development of Personality," *The Development of Personality,* CW 17, par. 286.

[17] "Transformation Symbolism in the Mass," *Psychology and Religion: West and East,* CW 11, par. 345.

that he was the "priest of the innermost hidden sanctuary." He then described how he had been torn apart, his bones and flesh reassembled, and then transformed into spirit through the process of burning. As this was told to Zosimos, the priest spewed forth his own flesh and changed into a manikin.

Here the priest left the established and collective sphere of the church, whereas the dreamer left the collective sphere of the state. Church and state can both be regarded as institutions which provide a maternal role when fulfilling their mandate to nourish their jurisdictions, though they do so through patriarchal structures. In much the same way the feminine basis to the aboriginal culture is managed by the patriarchy.

Once out of the church, the priest entered a solitary world under the ground. There, in true alchemical tradition, he presided over the transformation process and became both the sacrificer and the sacrificed. It was he who had to take the initiative by first entering the unconscious.

This is an example of how the individuation process requires one to be the priest of his or her own inner sanctum. This is what is required of the dreamer—to work with the small boy and bring him into consciousness. As with the mythological aboriginal boys, the bones and flesh have to be reconstituted, much as the transformation occurs in the vision when the priest spews forth the flesh or matter.

It has already been suggested that the myth represents the split in the aboriginal psyche. But it also represents the split in the white psyche. Here the diagram on page 65 reverses itself. The Dua is rejected and the Yiritja accepted, to the extent that the white man's identification with the Lumaluma figure is so strong that he is almost in a state of *participation mystique* with the principle Lumaluma represents. Hence the white man's predilection both to build structures and frameworks in which to orient himself, and to use the flying fox side to exclude the possibility of an intrusion from the feminine side of his psyche.

## The White Myth Makers

From the male-dominated myths concerning Laintjung, Lu'ningu and Lumaluma, the hypothesis was made that the emergence of white Australia as a nation was influenced by the same psychological dynamics that lead to a one-sided male consciousness. This is a state in which the flying foxes are in the ascendant while, at the same time, the homunculus and the feminine are suppressed.

By contrast, black Australia appears to have developed in such a manner that the principles symbolized by Lumaluma have been rejected in favor of a feminine dominant, as we saw in the Wawilak myth. To further investigate the manner in which Lumaluma re-emerged and took over the central position in the Australian psyche, we need only turn to the early white myth makers who promoted the spirit of Lumaluma while the land itself was devalued and its essential spirit ignored.

By the late nineteenth century, a hundred years after the first settlement, a rail network linked the country and political issues such as economic protection versus free trade, voting rights, as well as the insistence that colored immigration be disallowed, were being debated. Australian nationalism and the question of what it was to be an Australian were also being openly discussed for the first time. This was the beginning of an Australian consciousness and from the discussion of these political and identity issues, the Commonwealth of Australia was constituted in 1901.

Leading the "raising of consciousness" debate were two writers, Henry Lawson and A.B. Paterson. Vance Palmer captured the great influence they had on the national debate:

> Here . . . was the voice of the country, speaking through two different men, but with one recognizable accent. . . . The names of Lawson and Paterson are still so closely associated in the legend of the nineties that it is hard to prise them apart.[18]

---

18 *The Legend of the Nineties*, p. 109.

For the moment these two will be prised apart and the work of Lawson used as the metaphor which best illustrates the ambivalent feelings white Australians had toward their adopted country at the turn of the century. These feelings continue to be as problematic and confused today as they were at the birth of the nation.

Lawson, like the aboriginal myth makers, was a "swagman" or wanderer, and it was primarily from this perspective that he wrote about the nature of the land and his vision for the country. Although his literary abilities may be questioned,[19] few would disagree that he made a significant contribution to the country through his ability to encapsulate the images of what it was to be an Australian. As H.P. Eseltine expressed it, "He is revered as one of the greatest and most 'typically Australian' of our literary figures."[20]

Lawson had two views of the country. One was the small "b" bush, which he generally described in the most negative and pessimistic of terms. This view is succinctly summed up in his description of the country as an "Out Back Hell,"[21] and in desperate pleas such as "Oh, for God's sake take me away from the bush!"[22] Other similar phrases permeate his writings.[23] The reality of the bush repelled him and he saw it as a place which, if it were to be occupied, should be exploited for economic gain. This is reflected in "The Bush and the Ideal," in which he concluded that the salvation of the land was in its artificial development, hence his solution to the problem, "Let us irrigate."[24] This is the attitude that has continued to pre-

---

[19] See Judith Wright, "The Reformist Poets: Preoccupations in Australian Poetry," in C. Roderick, ed., *Henry Lawson: Criticism*, p. 393.

[20] "Saint Henry: Our Apostle of Mateship," ibid., p. 342. For similar sentiments see M. Dunlevy, "Lawson's Archetypes," ibid., p. 410; H.M. Green, *Lawson as Poet and Short Story Writer: A History of Australian Literature*, ibid., p. 350; C. Wallace-Crabbe, "Lawson's Joe Wilson."

[21] "Some popular Australian Mistakes," in C. Roderick, ed., *Henry Lawson: Autobiographical and Other Writings, 1887-1922*, vol. 2, p. 25.

[22] "The Selector's Daughter," in C. Roderick, ed., *Henry Lawson: Short Stories and Sketches*, vol. 1, p. 59.

[23] For example, see "Hungerford," ibid., p. 105.

[24] Roderick, *Autobiographical*, vol. 2, p. 32.

vail, with the extensive exploitation of the country's resources which today provides the basis for its economic structure.

From these few descriptions it is clear that for Lawson it was the negative side of Mother Nature that ruled the bush; her redeeming qualities apparently did not find their way to Australia. Lawson experienced only the ugly and destructive side of nature and as long as he assessed the environment through the standards of the English landscape,[25] he was effectively denying any positive potential that could emerge from the true spirit of the land.

In this regard Lawson's view characterized what Marie-Louise von Franz has described as *cognitio vespertina* or "evening knowledge."[26] This is a knowledge of life that is caught in the outer multiplicity of things, or a knowledge of things created, with the result that the individual becomes more and more removed from the inner knowledge of God. This is well represented by Lawson, who prided himself on his ability to see the country realistically and to describe situations accurately. It is the same Lawson who became enmeshed in the need to promote social and economic structures to satisfy the outer needs of man without any regard to his inner life. Significantly, he died a depressed alcoholic.

Von Franz contrasts evening knowledge to *cognitio matutina* or "morning knowledge," the awareness that the human being is made in the image of the Creator, a state in which the ego is expanded through contact with the Self. This was not Lawson; he completely ignored the native people in his writing and showed an inability to look into the meaning behind the phenomena he so colorfully described. His views were extraverted in that he looked out into the land and saw either its harshest qualities or values which would appeal to collective consciousness. In this way the emu as symbolizing the Earth Mother and the spirit of the land was kept in the realm "below," confined to the unconscious.

On the other hand, Lawson's capital "B" Bush was the Australia

---

[25] Ibid.

[26] *C.G. Jung: His Myth in Our Time,* chapt. 10.

of his vision that arose not from his experience of reality, but from an area that lay beyond the center of the country, the collective unconscious. This was the other side to the depressed view of the land which, for Lawson was

> A phantom land, a mystic realm!
> The Never Never Land.[27]

It was the realm in which heroes and ideas lived, and from which he saw such visions as the world of "Brotherhood and Love and Honour,"[28] and the Australian Republic rising from the ashes of war.[29] In this sphere the transcendental code of social conduct would be established. Here we meet the great Australian ethic of mateship, where each man would be equal to and the companion of the other. This notion arose from the belief that a single-handed attempt to deal with the bush would lead to a person's ruin; chances of survival would be better served by the system of mateship which, because of the collective premise on which it is based, would inevitably sacrifice the principle of individual initiative and development.

This is the land Lawson called "The Never Never Land," a place where the highest values would be manifested in the mythical Bushman, the white pioneer. As he succinctly stated in an article entitled "New Religion," mateship would be the basis of his concept of society and would be epitomized by "Trade unionism [as] a new and grand religion." [30]

From these few examples it can be seen that the notions which the Bush inspired were in the world of ideals, ideas, causes, political structures and collective organizations—the realm of Lumaluma. Lawson espoused the traditional Christian attitude toward nature, where only the collective altruistic notions she inspired were given value while the archaic religious messages that lay hidden in her were not even contemplated.

---

27 Roderick, *Criticism,* p. xxvii.

28 Ibid., p. xxiv.

29 "The Star of Australasia," *Winnowed Verses,* p. 2.

30 Roderick, *Autobiographical,* vol. 2, p. 16

Here the contrast between Lawson's attitude and the Aborigines' is striking because they revered her to such an extent that their lives were organized around the mystery gods of nature. Jung once observed that the Christian world had striven to alienate itself from its instincts to such an extent that it saw nature as being abhorrent.[31] He referred to St. Augustine, who said, "And men go forth, and admire lofty mountains and broad seas, . . . and turn away from themselves."[32] In a similar manner this is what Lawson did when he got caught in the lofty ideals inspired by his Never Never Land, while at the same time showing a remarkable ability to completely ignore its myths and inner message.

Lawson's notions were projections of ideals from the unconscious, with no grounding in reality. He took flight from the real world, which he saw in the most miserable of lights of the negative mother principle, and escaped into the comfort of paradisiacal ideas. In this context the emu, which is a flightless bird, would represent ideas that could remain grounded and tied to reality. In addition we have already seen from another myth that the emu responds to the moment, and makes no contribution to the codification of ideals. As a result, she was kept below in the dark, along with Yurlunggur, while the spirit of Lumaluma prevailed.

The inspiration Lawson received from the Bush is symptomatic of the prevailing masculine-Christian principle; it is a world where the flying fox is in the ascendant, dominating the young masculine and the emu. As long as this principle rules, the frail boy symbolizing the homunculus, or personal godhead, would be neglected. In this case, rather than developing a personal relationship with such a figure, he was projected into the ideals that lie in the Never Never Land. This inevitably resulted in him being only a collective concept and one which will "Never" be realized.

The weakness of developing ideas in a state of religious fervor has been described by Jung in the following manner:

---

[31] *Symbols of Transformation,* CW 5, pars. 106-107.
[32] Ibid., par. 107.

> The *unconscious* conversion of instinctual impulses into religious activity is ethically worthless, and often no more than an hysterical outburst, even though its products may be aesthetically valuable.[33]

This seems to be what happened to Lawson. Unconscious instinctual impulses were projected onto collective ideals such as trade unionism. While trade unionism reflects a valued collective ethic, the fact that he saw it as a new religion suggests that its conceptualization was not based in reality. Such an inflated response can result when the archetype is not differentiated from the object; in this case the archetype of the Self became enmeshed in a social goal.

Lawson's psychological relationship with the Bush can also be seen as an example of a "dual focus" in the psyche, in that besides ego-consciousness there is the collective unconscious. "A second psychic system," wrote Jung, "coexist[s] with consciousness."[34] The question therefore arises as to who or what in Lawson espoused his views.

One can postulate that it was the unconscious speaking and that he missed an opportunity to become conscious of the source in his psyche of such fantasies and dreams. Instead, he left them in Never Never Land. There was certainly a split in his view of the land. On the one hand, it was a very negative experience, while on the other he expressed its value through the most altruistic of constructs and through the type of inflated language typical of spontaneous outbursts from the unconscious. "The neurotic," wrote Jung, "is . . . [a] disunited man who ought to harmonise nature and culture within himself."[35] Lawson valued culture to such an extent that instincts and nature were only felt in their negativity, leaving his soul divided. It was he who originated the phrase, "Sydney or the bush."

In contrast to the collective heroes of the Bush, the (small "b") bush heroes were invariably solitary figures who found it impossible

---

[33] Ibid., par. 106.

[34] "On the Nature of the Psyche," *The Structure and Dynamics of the Psyche,* CW 8, par. 369.

[35] "On the Psychology of the Unconscious," *Two Essays on Analytical Psychology,* CW 7, par. 16.

to sustain relations in civilized society. These are the men who found that an attachment to a wife crippled them, and there are many stories and poems where the wife is left behind and forced to fend for herself.[35] This inability to relate to the "other" is reflected in Lawson's poem about the bush hero as the singular, lonely male who is incapable of relationship:

> They smile and are not happy;
> They sing and are not gay;
> They weary, yet they wander;
> They love, and cannot stay;
> They marry, and are single
> Who watch the roving star,
> For, by the family fireside
> O lonely men they are![36]

That he is isolated and lonely is only to be expected, since the anima is left behind and forgotten, confined to the unconscious. As Lawson simply expressed it, the bush was "no place for a woman."[37] In his schema the women would stay at home in the locale from which the husband started his journey. As a wanderer, like the seafarers who brought the settlers on their six-month journey to Australia, the swagman continued this tradition on land. He personified longing, in this case longing for the lost mother.

Ironically, the woman left behind symbolizes the feminine spirit which could lead a man out of isolation and into a relationship with life, by taking him from the world of the flying foxes and Lumaluma's lifeless skeletal structure, into the unconscious where waits his true potential. Instead she is abandoned, stereotyped into a collective function. Eros stays underground, precluding the possibility of complete masculine development. For the masculine principle to reach its potential, an easy relationship with the feminine must be established. With Lumaluma in charge a person is not capable of de-

---

[35] See, for example, Lawson, "The Drover's Wife," in Roderick, *Autobiographical,* vol. 1, p. 47.

[36] Roderick, *Criticism,* pp. xxix-xxx.

[37] "The Bush Undertaker," in Roderick, *Autobiographical,* vol. 1, pp. 52ff.

veloping positive personal relationships.

It was from a view of the country such as that championed by Lawson that the Commonwealth of Australia came into being. Not surprisingly, its Coat of Arms reflects some of these attitudes.

The kangaroo is commonly regarded as a male figure in aboriginal mythology,[38] while we have already seen that the emu is considered female. In a positive sense these two instinctual figures are the opposites holding together the union of the six states. Linking the whole picture is the vegetative spirit of the country, Mother Nature herself in the form of the national flower, the golden wattle. Plant life is an appropriate symbol for the unfolding spirit of the individual as well as the spirit of an individual country. Rising over this union is the five-pointed Star of Australia, the quintessence of the union. The image is reminiscent of the alchemical pictures from the *Rosarium philosophorum*,[39] particularly the one reproduced here as "The

---

[38] See Warner, *A Black Civilization*, pp. 302ff, and C. Mountford, "The Rainbow-Serpent Myths of Australia," in I.R. Buchler and K. Maddock, *The Rainbow Serpent*, pp. 23-98.

[39] "The Psychology of the Transference," *The Practice of Psychotherapy*, CW 16, pars. 402ff.

Naked Truth." It shows conscious and unconscious linked through the hands of king and queen (Sol and Luna), representing a *coniunctio* mediated by the Holy Spirit.

The Naked Truth.

In the Coat of Arms, an important duality is missing. There is no living link with the unconscious because the two stems of wattle have been coldly cut, leaving the plant floating and not grounded. We are left with the image of a plant doomed not to grow to full maturity, a situation in which the *principium individuonis* (the tree) has no chance of life. Although the animals are in an apparent relationship in the upper realm, there is no contact or union with the lower, as would be necessary for a healthy relationship. By contrast the image of the Naked Truth is firmly grounded by the figures having contact with their psychological opposite.

The five-pointed star completes the picture of a traditional Christian Trinity, representing the masculine dominance of church and state. Thus the Coat of Arms depicts a relationship involving only a superficial fascination, cold and impersonal; no deep mingling of souls is possible when there is no ground in which the relationship can grow. It is as if it were only a marriage of convenience, which is close to the fact, because the states came together mainly to protect themselves rather than out of a deep love for a common vision.

A Coat of Arms related to the true spirit of the land would be well rooted in the collective unconscious. What better images to include in the national symbol than the Wawilaks and Yurlunggur?

Here the masculine kangaroo would have the Wawilaks as the feminine in his unconscious while the emu would have the masculine aspects of Yurlunggur. At both the conscious and unconscious levels there would be a union of opposites; a marriage quaternio would be created, linked by the creative vegetative spirit in the form of the golden wattle. The result is a mandala, symbol of an inner bond able to withstand outside forces that could threaten the country—or an individual—with disintegration.

**4**

# The Alien Man

In the previous chapters comments were made on the psychological dynamics involved in the split between the black and white Australian collectives.

On the one hand there are the Aborigines who have a strong identity with the land and pay homage to their nature gods through their myths and rituals. At the same time they appear to devalue and deny the principle of Logos which, after being suppressed for thousands of years, was to eventually manifest itself as the white invasion. On the other hand is the white culture and some of its myth makers who wandered through the land contemplating principles associated with the patriarchy (utopias, causes and "isms"), yet failing to make contact with the innate spirit of the land. In this sense they epitomized the deficiencies in the Christian ethos to which Jung has referred throughout his writings, namely an absence of the feminine principle, a suppression of the dark side of the psyche and a denial of the nature basis of Christianity.[1]

The repression of the opposite principle in each culture resulted in one-sidedness. Only collective attitudes prevailed because of an overidentification with archetypes. Each precluded the presence of an "other" and hence no tension was created from which a third attitude or transcendent function could emerge. For the Murngin the effect was that the rules of the Dua prevailed, while in the white culture it was the spirit of Lumaluma that was dominant. The collective celebration of these respective forces has also given a distinctive stamp to individual members. Whereas both cultures support collective attitudes at the expense of the individual, one is characterized more by the feminine principle, the other more by the masculine.

---

1 See, for example, *Aion*, CW 9ii, pars. 267ff, and *Psychology and Alchemy*, CW 12, pars. 447ff..

81

This chapter examines a process through which these two divergent attitudes are integrated by one individual—an individuated person emerging from the collective. It focuses on the making of a medicine-man in Australia, particularly on an example from the Wuradjeri tribe.[2] It demonstrates how a psychic split is bridged through the medicine-man's ability to develop a relationship with the archetypal world of the feminine, as represented by the Rainbow Serpent, and the archetypal world of the father, represented by the masculine sky god Baiame. Through his courage to withstand the tension of these opposites, he is able to disidentify from their collective aspects and emerge with the individual spirit of each. Because of his efforts the two worlds are integrated by and in him.

## Making a Medicine-Man

Throughout Australia, there is no single way by which a medicine-man is made, and even within a tribe the process can vary. However there are generic themes which involve proving his innate special qualities, such as the ability to have a number of ecstatic or spiritual experiences and the capacity to produce quartz or some other magical substance from his body.

Once he has passed such tests, he then receives powers which can only be bestowed through a personal meeting with the supernatural spirit. The result of this process is that he lives in two worlds, the tribal and the sacred world of the beginning. Through his contact with the world of consciousness and that of the archetypes, he assumes the role of intermediary between the tribe and its heroes. By actively and creatively integrating the mystery of the unconscious into his conscious life he becomes the symbol of the *principium individuonis*.

The making of a medicine-man in the Wuradjeri tribe has three

---

2 The Wuradjeri Rainbow Serpent also swallows humans and plays the central role in initiation rituals. See M.J. Meggit, "Gadjeri Among the Walbiri Aborigines of Central Australia."

stages.[3] The first occurs during the postulant's youth when he is selected on the simple basis of the elders' intuition that he has a predilection for the "other world," that is, the unconscious. He is then trained by his father and must prove himself in a number of areas. The most significant involves receiving quartz into his body, either through drinking water that contains quartz crystals or having the quartz "sung" into him. Some months or even years later, he must prove his worthiness to proceed to the next stage by physically removing the particles from his body. During this phase, he must also report experiences of seeing ghosts.

Once these tasks have been fulfilled, the great god Baiame indicates to his father in a dream that the boy will be received by him. The postulant is then given a totem of a patrilineal snake spirit, in addition to the ordinary, matrilineal totem he received when he went through the normal age-grading ceremony.[4] It is as if through the earlier initiation he made contact with images of the mother archetype (the nature gods) whereas now it is his fate to follow a path which will lead him to images of the father.

As is appropriate where there is a prevailing feminine psychology, it is the masculine psychopomp in its primeval form, the patrilineal snake totem, which leads him into the world of darkness. Here the light (quartz) must guide him along his individual path. He meets many Daramulums who are the sons of Baiame. By proving his ability to see them, he is rewarded by receiving wisdom after having a snake rubbed against him.

In another version, rather than meeting the Daramulums, Baiame himself drags the postulant from his familiar tribal land to a cave in a strange country and imparts secrets to him—from the world of conventional and collective consciousness to a place of irrationality from which he will be reborn.

---

[3] See A.P. Elkin, *Aboriginal Men of High Degree*, pp. 83-87; A.W. Howitt, *The Native Tribes of South-East Australia*, pp. 405-408; R.M. Berndt, "Wuradjeri Magic and Clever Men," pp. 332-338.

[4] Berndt, "Wuradjeri Magic," p. 333.

After experiencing this underground world, he climbs to the sky on a cord produced from his testes or his perineum (the versions vary). To make the ascent he must pass through a number of layers which open and close very quickly.[5] Should he be touched by one of them, he would fail as a prospective medicine-man and have to return home. Once he has successfully negotiated these layers he enters the remarkable world of Baiame, who has quartz coming from his shoulders, sits on a quartz throne and has light coming from his eyes. At this point the postulant's arms are made into feathered wings and the medicine-man's secrets are conveyed to him. One of these secrets is that Baiame is the source of all earthly quartz and that quartz is "solidified light." The new medicine-man then returns home to assume his responsibilities in the tribe.

The nature of the substance initially absorbed by the postulant varies throughout Australia. It could be in the form of snakes, stones or pearls, but most often it is quartz. In the Wuradjeri tradition quartz is the magic substance and we are told not only of its source (Baiame's throne) but that it represents solidified light. The common qualities of light and quartz are therefore linked and, in this context, they can be seen as both being normally white and at the same time containing all the colors. Similarly, pearls too possess the quality of having all the colors in one body, as well as being water-born.

Another natural phenomenon that contains the seven colors as well as being the form in which water and light are united is the rainbow, which links the opposite environments of heaven and earth. These phenomena symbolize the key motif in our central myth, the

---

[5] This is a variation of the "clashing rocks" motif common to heroic, funerary and shamanic mythologies in different parts of the world. The dangerous passage to the "other world" is envisioned variously as dancing, razor-sharp reeds; snapping jaws of monstrous animals; opening and closing waters (e.g., the flight of the Jews from Egypt into the Promised Land); shifting islands (or, among the Eskimos, icebergs); and other versions of the classic Symplegades (rocks) that threatened to crush the Argonauts. Among the North American Huichol Indians, the dangerous passage is called "the Gateway of the Clashing Clouds." (See Peter T. Furst, "The Shamanic Universe," p. 43)

Rainbow Serpent, whose body contains all the colors and whose realm is water.

From these associations it can be concluded that quartz, the source of the medicine-man's power, symbolizes the Rainbow Serpent.[6] The postulant's power is derived from his ability to incorporate and then produce the Rainbow Serpent from his body, his own matter. The end result is that the earth-bound quartz-Rainbow Serpent is personalized both by and through the postulant. The individual spirit of the Rainbow Serpent is redeemed through him, and the remainder of the process tells us more about the nature of the snake's individual spirit. In other words the postulant becomes the medium through which the Rainbow Serpent can express its individual nature, just as it was through the tribe that the deity was able to express its collective nature. Thus the macrocosm and the microcosm are redeemed through the actions of an individual.

If left to the initiative of the community, the ceremonies involving the Rainbow Serpent would always end with the deity returning to the realm of the maternal underworld, only to reappear for the same cycle of rituals the next time. As a result the ceremonies never change significantly; like the climatic seasons on which they are based, the same patterns are repeated during each cycle.

The repetitive nature of the rituals reflects a psychological situation in which the outer psychic condition is neither changing nor developing. Further, since the ceremonies take place in a collective milieu and occur at the behest of the tribal elders, they reflect not only a situation where the same conscious attitude prevails but also an attitude that has become stuck because other possibilities have not been entertained. In other words, should the contents from the unconscious remain repressed and not integrated into consciousness, the same stale patterns will prevail.

As long as the Rainbow Serpent remains at the bottom of the collective well, he will symbolize the closed ring of the uroboros snake rather than a more open system which would be represented by, for

---

[6] Elkin, *Aboriginal Men,* pp. 82-88.

example, the Kundalini snake. As a result the Rainbow Serpent in his underground world will represent the atavistic tendency which holds our psychic energy in a primordial, inert state, where the integration of new attitudes (Lu'ningu in the case of the Aborigines) will be resisted. In other words the complex, in the form of the strong maternal presence, blocks the flow of energy, leading to a lack of development in both the individual and the collective. The feeling-tone associated with this situation is well expressed by a commentary on Hexagram 18 of the I Ching, where stagnation is described as a state of "gentle indifference" and "rigid inertia."[7]

## Searching Within

By extracting the quartz-Rainbow Serpent from his body, the postulant takes the symbol out of the collective realm and into the personal. As a result he can no longer identify himself with the collective; rather he adopts an individual attitude toward the Rainbow Serpent for which he will ultimately be rewarded when he receives its transforming power and becomes a medicine-man.

This inspired individual action is also the basis for personal transformation in the Gnostic and alchemical traditions. By comparing their processes with that of the postulant, we can develop a better sense of the possible meaning behind the medicine-man's development, as well as gain a deeper appreciation of the mysterious phenomena that link the divergent cultures of the West and the Aborigines.

The motifs for this link appear in a dream mentioned earlier (page 32), where Jung presented the dreamer with a block of iron to work on; that is, he had to become conscious of its symbolic value. While Jung challenged him to become acquainted with the *opus alchymicum*, an aboriginal woman gave him the symbol of the quartz-Rainbow Serpent in the form of a tie.

Meteorites, composed of magnetite and hematite, are an unrefined

---

[7] *The I Ching or Book of Changes,* p. 75.

form of iron ore. Historically, they have inspired awe and reverence because they were considered to be both a message from the alien world and a representation of the sanctity of heaven.[8] In much the same way rock crystals or quartz were regarded as materials from the heavenly throne and were held in awe by Aborigines. The quartz-Rainbow Serpent contains the opposites, having a grounded, feminine quality (residing within the earth) as well as an aerial and masculine quality (derived from the light and the god).

Toward the end of the Wawilak myth, Yurlunggur made an undifferentiated or unconscious union with the Wawilaks when he swallowed them. They were locked in the darkness of his body until he vomited them up. The archetype of the *coniunctio* or union of opposites was constellated, but fell into the world of unconsciousness by virtue of Yurlunggur returning to the well. It is as if he entered a world unknowable to the psyche, namely the psychoid world of the instincts and physical processes.[9] Here the process became stuck. In alchemy, the *filius* or transformed Mercurius would have emerged from this union and a new light born. ("It is the aim of alchemy to beget this light in the shape of the *filius philosophorum.*")[10] The intent of the adept was to free the divine soul, the *anima mundi*, which was bound up in the prison of matter. In a similar vein the postulant acts as an alchemist when he seeks the Rainbow Serpent, symbolized by the quartz, in the matter of his own body.

It will be recalled that in a dream referred to earlier (page 58), the dreamer was lowered into a circular pit or *nanggaru*, after leaving the patriarchal world (the high school) which he felt had absorbed his ego. It will also be recalled that the pit contained feathers and stones. These are archetypal symbols which an understanding of mythology and ritual can help amplify. It will also be recalled that the dreamer had pronounced somatic problems. Thus, through motifs similar to

---

[8] M. Eliade, *The Forge and the Crucible*, p. 27.

[9] See "On the Nature of the Psyche," *The Structure and Dynamics of the Psyche*, CW 8, pars. 368ff.

[10] "Paracelsus As a Spiritual Phenomenon," *Alchemical Studies*, CW 13, par. 161.

those that appear in the making of a medicine-man, the dreamer is being led toward greater body consciousness, encouraged to discover the deepest spiritual principle that resides in his own matter. In a similar vein the snake tie in the other dream is analogous to the quartz in that it is a constant reminder of the relationship between matter and spirit.

Collectively the Aborigines would never dive into the Mirrirmina well where Yurlunggur lived, for fear of being eaten by him. The individual hero disregards these collective rules when he spontaneously goes into his own undifferentiated matter to rescue the quartz-Rainbow Serpent. By diving into his well of unconsciousness he initiates a process through which he will eventually develop a personal relationship with the godhead. Similarly, the dreamer will have to enter the realm of which he is most unconscious, his body or feminine principle, if he is to develop a grounded spiritual attitude.

The medicine-man produces quartz from his body and the new light is born. Appropriately it is produced in a concrete form. As Jung has observed, "Every archetype, before it is integrated consciously, wants to manifest itself physically."[11] The concrete manifestation would be the act of producing quartz, however this could also be regarded as a metaphor for psychosomatic and physical reactions. According to Jung, the instinctual world is somehow connected with the psyche through physical processes;[12] thus psychosomatic reactions would be derived from the psychoid world of instincts. In this context, the production of quartz would represent the first step by which a connection is made between the worlds of the body and the psyche, instinct and archetype. The experience of the postulant reflects this in that the inspiration for him to embark on a path of individuation is derived from below the floor of the well.

The appearance of the quartz is effectively equivalent to a somatic

---

[11] *C.G. Jung Letters,* vol. 1, p. 336.

[12] "On the Nature of the Psyche," *The Structure and Dynamics of the Psyche,* CW 8, pars. 343ff; see also Marie-Louise von Franz, *Puer Aeternus: A Psychological Study of the Adult Struggle with the Paradise of Childhood,* p. 147.

reaction, but the real meaning at this point would appear to be only an idea or intuition. Bringing it to greater consciousness will require further processing. "So must he [Mercurius] be raised from the earth and cleansed of all earthiness, then he ascends entire into thin air, and is changed into spirit."[13] Despite the appearance of the quartz, the postulant's conscious attitude would still be governed by the same laws of nature that are conscious to the tribe and he would only have an intuitive knowledge of the importance of his discovery.

There is a parallel here with the alchemical notion of the "light of nature," which Paracelsus described as "an intuitive apprehension of the fact, a kind of illumination."[14] He postulated two sources of knowledge, the light of nature, *lumen naturae,* which was temporal, and the light of revelation which was eternal. These he related to the two life forces in man, the natural and the aerial, both of which took their light from the one god. For Paracelsus, the *lumen naturae* was the divine spark buried in the darkness; in this sense, it is equivalent to the solidified light buried in the medicine-man. However it was not merely a product of nature as we know it, "not from flesh and blood . . . but from the stars in flesh and blood."[15] Similarly the postulant's solidified light did not originate in his body but had its source in the sky god, Baiame.

For the Gnostics also, the fate of light was a central motif. Gnosis means knowledge of, or insight into, the divine essence of man.[16] It refers not to rational knowledge but wisdom achieved through a personal experience of the Self. Gnosticism taught that to know the deepest level of oneself was to know God and only this would lead to salvation. The emphasis was on experience rather than faith. For the Gnostic, the revelation would be solely at the behest of God and through the appearance of his messenger. This Gnostic God, like the

---

13 Penotus, *Theatrum chemicum,* I (1659), quoted by Jung in "The Spirit Mercurius," *Alchemical Studies,* par. 279.

14 "Paracelsus As a Spiritual Phenomenon," ibid., par. 148.

15 Ibid., par. 149.

16 H. Jonas, *The Gnostic Religion,* p. 32.

aboriginal god who lived in the sky beyond Baiame, was absolutely transmundane and unknowable; again it fits the description of Jung's concept of the psychoid, but this time the sky god would represent the unknowable world of the father archetype. As a result, the perception of such a concept could only be hypothesized through the archetype's image. One of these images is the messenger of God or Alien Man.

The Gnostics viewed the world and universe negatively, seeing it as a place of darkness, wickedness and evil. Trapped in this world and, in particular, within the body, was the spark of divine light which had originated outside the universe but had fallen into this world and become imprisoned. This is analogous to the spiritual center or Self being kept from consciousness by an ego which refuses to recognize the possibility of an authority greater than itself.

The notion of the spark being trapped in the world of matter appears in the following man's dream.

> I am sitting in the back of a church where there are four women. The fourth is an elderly aboriginal woman. She explains that she is able to see sparks of light in the church and that they bounce off the walls. Her description is so vivid that I am also able to picture them. She then takes hold of me and tells me she will take me to her world.

Here we find a number of motifs similar to those that appear in the making of a medicine-man. The central image is that of sparks of light being trapped in the church which, if seen as Mother Church, highlights the fact that the divine spark is caught in matter and cannot escape—the entrapped spark of the Gnostics caught in the world of collective darkness.

This image is akin to the personal quartz still being in the darkness of the postulant's body, and also reflects the collective state where the Rainbow Serpent is still at the bottom of the well, a sleeping uroboros. As long as a condition such as this prevails, the conventional approach to religion will remain undisturbed because the spark of life cannot be seen—the spark representing the inner man of the alchemists, the light of the God of the Gnostics, the quartz of the

Aborigines, and also Christ in the Christian tradition ("I am the light of the world").[17]

In the dream the figure representing the Great Mother is prepared to tell the dreamer about this inner secret of matter from a perspective similar to that of the alchemists, who saw matter as being not only body but also spirit. This is in marked contrast to the perspective that the congregation or collective would have had of Mother Church because the living spirit was invisible to them. The congregation could only see an empty space.

In a similar manner, the orthodox development of an aboriginal boy meant that, at a prescribed time, he would be introduced into the secrets of his tribe which he would share with the other adults. Through such a practice he became a member of the tribal congregation, believing in those concepts and practices that had been accepted for generations. In terms of the above dream this would be equivalent to the church congregation unquestioningly accepting the collective ritual. However the process in the making of the medicine-man indicates a way by which this unconscious pattern can be broken. This is seen when the aboriginal boy is blessed with the ecstatic experience of producing quartz; once he has had this experience, he is put on a path leading to another dimension of life, that is, an aspect other than the collective one with which he previously identified.

A similar challenge is presented in the dream where the aboriginal woman inspires the dreamer to envision the sparks bouncing off the walls. In effect, she introduces him to the possibility of a religious life invisible to the collective. The fact that it is she who is able to stimulate his vision also suggests the process of active imagination, which to be successful requires the participation of the anima. Through her guidance the dreamer is led into a special or unknown world in much the same way as Baiame guides the postulant into a dark land and initiates him into the secrets of the medicine-man.

This Earth Mother is the fourth woman in the church, suggesting that she represents the inferior function, the one farthest from con-

---

[17] John 8:12, Revised Standard Version.

sciousness. Certainly she would be the fourth or weakest function of
the contemporary church, since she is dark, female and related to nature, aspects of life the church has long suppressed. Just as she will
take the dreamer into her world, so the postulant is taken into the underworld to start a new stage of life.

It is as if, up to this point, the postulant's experience represented a
person's development in the first half of life where, typically, emphasis is on adaptation to the collective and the body, in addition to
the occasional suggestion that another, magical world might exist
(for instance, the production of the quartz). However now the second half of life beckons; the ego begins to lose its feeling of absolute
power and a sense develops that an unknown "other" requires attention. It is this "other" that becomes restless in the postulant and will
lead him into a more conscious awareness of the spirit world.

This part of the process begins when he is led underground. Here
there are no familiar points of orientation; by virtue of being taken
into this dark and unknown world, his usual conscious viewpoint is
lost and he is forced to rely on the intuitive qualities of his light
(quartz) to guide him through the ordeal. Here he also meets the
Daramulums which, because of their large numbers, further suggests
that at this stage he has only an inkling of the power of Baiame; that
is, his image of the sky god is undifferentiated and disunited. The
postulant's task, then, will be to differentiate and integrate the god
through his personal experience.

When he goes underground he symbolically enters the unconscious. Being immersed in the earth would refer particularly to the
experience of suffering through those painful and regrettable qualities
associated with the personal shadow. The holes he has to go through
during this stage would therefore represent the successive layers of
his shadow. His safe passage through them would result in a pro-
gressively greater state of consciousness. Once he has gone through
this difficult experience he is rewarded by receiving wisdom from the
snake. We are not told what constitutes this wisdom; perhaps it is related to the Rainbow Serpent now becoming a living entity rather
than the abstract, intuitive notion it was when perceived as quartz.

Whatever the specific details, the process is psychologically apt in that a differentiation is made between the world of darkness, or the shadow, and the world of the spirit. In other words, the underground experience represents a process through which shadow contents are integrated by the ego, while the snake-spirit is recognized as belonging to the nonpersonalized aspect of the psyche, the collective unconscious.[18]

With the personal and the impersonal differentiated, there will be little danger of the postulant becoming inflated during the remaining part of the journey, nor of identifying with the archetype he is about to meet. Should he identify with it he would simply enter a state similar to that which enmeshes the tribe; however in his case he would be caught up in a *participation mystique* with the masculine spirit in contrast to the tribe's identification with the feminine world. When he is eventually confronted by the spirit of the godhead, his ability to discriminate between the personal and impersonal will enable him to recognize that it is God speaking through him rather than believing he is God.

## The Cord

After the postulant has gone through the personal suffering involved in the underground experience, he emerges with a more creative attitude, represented by the cord he spontaneously produces from his body. In some tribes the cord is produced from the stomach while in others, as happens with the Wuradjeri, it comes from the genitals.

It will be recalled that in the previous phase the postulant made contact with the living snake, indicating that it became a differentiated part of his personal reality. Now, in the form of the cord, it seems as if the snake is being brought into the outer or conscious realm via the body of the postulant. The process by which it is brought above ground and into the more conscious realm is through an act of projection. Symbolically this indicates that a part of himself is projected,

---

[18] *Psychology and Alchemy,* CW 12, par. 242n.

representing a process conceptually similar to a form of active imagination whereby psychic energy that has been held in the body is released and allowed to flow along its natural course. When the postulant produces the cord it is as if he were listening to his somatic reactions caused by the restlessness of the snake, and is prepared to follow them in his imagination in order to find out where the wisdom of the snake wants to lead him.

We are then told that the snake's energy wants to lead the postulant toward the upper world of the father spirits. In other words, the libido seeks to break the enclosed ring of the uroboros, here symbolizing a collective and stagnating life, and create a living and individual dimension. This extra meaning can only be realized when his energy moves and begins to link his instinctual and spiritual worlds, those of the mother and father archetypes, Dua and Yiritja.

We can approach the meaning of all this through a dream in which an old man told the dreamer, an Australian, to cross a bridge.

> I followed the old man's advice and entered a land that had a strange feeling to it. On the edge of a shore were a large number of green shrimp and from them a multicolored rope arose, the main colors being red and dark blue. I then saw an aboriginal man standing next to the rope and thought that he must have emerged from it.

Just as in the making of a medicine-man the postulant is taken into a strange land by Baiame and told some of his secrets, here the dreamer is directed by a wise old man to enter the land of the Aborigine via a bridge linking the two cultures.

In this land the rope rises from the unconscious, represented by a sea of shrimp. In the dream they are green, although in reality shrimp also contain muted other colors not unlike the hues that appear in a pearl. Also, because they are crustacean and early forms of development, they can be seen as a primeval representation of the Rainbow Serpent. Like the Daramulums, there are many of them, suggesting an undifferentiated version of the great deity. The dream describes the same situation that appears in the Wuradjeri making—having seen the shrimp-Daramulums, the cord symbolizing the Rainbow

Serpent rises from the unconscious, represented by water in the dream and as the underground in the Wuradjeri initiation.

The association of the cord in the dream with the Rainbow Serpent is reinforced by the image of the multicolored rope, the predominant colors of which are red and blue. This description conjures up the image of light when it is passed through a prism, producing a range of colors with red at one end and blue at the other. Significantly, Jung used the color spectrum as a metaphor to explain the connection between body and psyche, instinct and archetype.[19]

| **INSTINCT** | **ARCHETYPE** |
|---|---|
| infrared ———————————————————— ultraviolet | |
| (**Physiological:** body symptoms, instinctual perceptions, etc.) | (**Psychological:** spirit, dreams, conceptions, images, fantasies, etc.) |

The red aspect of the rope is the infrared pole of the spectrum, connected with physical processes and somatic reactions, symbolized by producing quartz and the cord from the body. This is the earthy realm where the quartz-Rainbow Serpent resides.

The rope also contains the dark blue or ultraviolet end of the spectrum, which Jung associated with the archetypes. Because archetypes are experienced in the form of images, this end of the spectrum would be the source of the fantasy/active imagination of the cord being projected into the sky. Thus the image of the rope reinforces what is being bridged by the postulant, namely the world of instinct and archetype.

Discussing Jung's metaphor, Marie-Louise von Franz writes:

Ego consciousness is like a ray of light, with a nucleus in it to represent the ego, which is a kind of field of light that can shift along the spectrum. . . . At the one end is the body, and at the other are the ideas and representations that suddenly seize upon the human mind.

---

19 "On the Nature of the Psyche," *The Structure and Dynamics of the Psyche,* CW 8, pars. 384ff.

Generally, our consciousness shifts between the two poles.[20]

Overall, the dream suggests the need for the two realms to be embraced by a conscious attitude if the split between them is to be healed. The ego is not only the link between the two worlds, it also mediates and holds the tension between them.

Jung observed that Eros has two sides: on one hand it belongs to mankind's primordial animal nature and on the other it is related to the highest form of the spirit.

> [Eros] thrives only when spirit and instinct are in right harmony. If one or the other aspect is lacking. . . the result is injury or at least a lopsidedness that may easily veer towards the pathological. Too much of the animal distorts the civilized man, too much civilization makes sick animals.[21]

Thus we can also see the cord as an image of balance, with neither the instincts of the Wawilaks nor the structural world of the father being overdominant. That it is produced from the testicles-perineum, anatomically the creative source, suggests that the individual journey along the cord will demand spontaneous and creative energy if the postulant is to succeed in bridging the two realms. This challenge is similar to that undertaken by the yogi in the Kundalini system, where the starting point is the *muladhara* chakra.[22]

In *muladhara* the yellow earth or square contains all the elements including the yoni or womb, which in turn contains the lingam, symbolizing the universal masculine principle, Shiva. In this chakra the feminine principle dominates and the masculine is unconscious, in much the same way as we have seen with the Aborigines. As long as this state prevails, a creative meeting of the opposites will be thwarted and the atavistic tendency will continue. For the yogi this plane represents a state in which there is no zeal for life, simply a lethargic hanging on to existence—rigid inertia and gentle indiffer-

---

[20] *Puer Aeternus,* p. 147.

[21] "On the Psychology of the Unconscious," *Two Essays on Analytical Psychology,* CW 7, par. 32.

[22] See Joseph Campbell, *The Mythic Image,* p. 341.

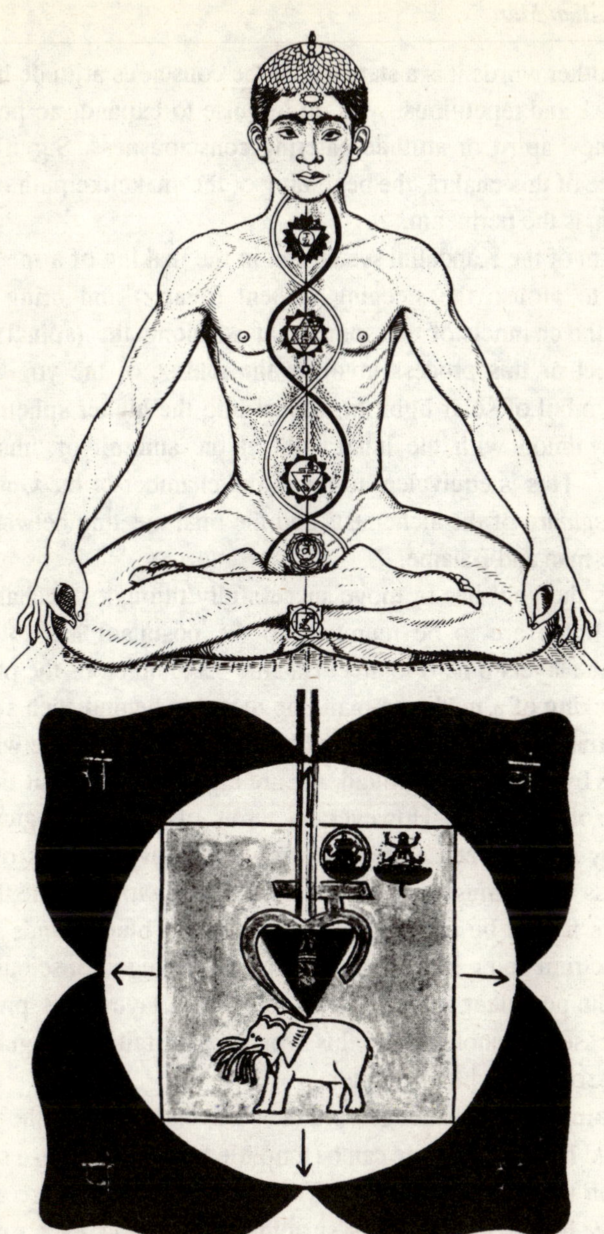

*Top:* The seven lotus centers of the Kundalini.
*Bottom:* *Muladhara,* the lowest chakra.
(From Joseph Campbell, *The Mythic Image*)

ence. In other words it is a state where the conscious attitude has become stuck and repetitious, with no impulse to expand, no possibility of a new spirit or attitude entering consciousness. Significantly the source of this chakra, the beginning of the snakelike path of individuation, is the perineum.

The aim of the Kundalini system, as in the making of a medicine-man, is to arouse the sleeping serpent (quartz) and bring it up through the channels of the spine, that is, along the (spinal) cord. One aspect of this process involves the release of the yogi's own *shakti,* symbol of solar light, for ascent into the higher spheres and ultimately union with the lunar light at the summit or "marriage chamber." This is equivalent to the bridal chamber of the Gnostics, the *hierosgamos* of the alchemists and the final meeting between the medicine-man and Baiame.

Just as the yogi has to move successfully through the chakras if the two lights are to be reunited, so the postulant has to move through the layers if he is to meet Baiame. Like much of the process in the making of a medicine-man, the meaning behind each stage is not explained. Just as we are not told about the nature of the wisdom he attains by going underground, we are also not told about the significance of the layers. However, in terms of a psychological process, they can be seen as representing successive degrees of consciousness which must be achieved if he is finally to integrate the sky god. This would be equivalent to the red and blue strands in the rope-spectrum being increasingly integrated by ego consciousness. Should the postulant be touched by one of the layers, his progress would cease. Psychologically this would be to fail to integrate the energy associated with a complex.

The nature of the challenges and the particular elements the postulant would have to integrate can be amplified by considering a similar process in the Gnostic tradition. The Gnostics' layers were *aeons,* successive hostile realms which surrounded the world, each ruled by an archon who had the responsibility to maintain *heimarmene* or universal fate. In other words, the archon's task was to ensure that conventional and established societal rules were maintained, and that the individual perpetuate and remain identified with collective consciousness. This the archon could do only by preventing the individual from continuing on his personal quest.[23]

To overcome the archon, the pneumatic[24] would have to trick him or use some other creative ploy, in much the same way that the postulant has to react quickly if he is to avoid touching the edge of one of the layers. In effect, the responses of both pneumatic and postulant represent the essence of what constitutes a creative life, one in which each moment is met spontaneously and naturally.

According to the *Poimandres,* the challenges to be met at each successive *aeon* include overcoming "evil machinations, lust, power, riches, lie, rash audacity."[25] These suggest that psychologically the challenge is to integrate different aspects of the shadow and, more specifically, to come to terms with values generally espoused in the first half of life, such as economic and professional success. The added implication is that one has to turn away from collective, extraverted values. Each successive movement through an *aeon* would then represent a more pronounced degree of introversion; one would be turned inward, focus of the second stage of life.

Another aspect to this phase may reflect the greatest challenge to those seeking the path to individuation. In the making of a medicine-man, the act of climbing the cord is witnessed by members of the tribe and there are many first-hand accounts of such an ascent.[26] Expressed in equivalent European terms, his professional development comes under public scrutiny. Should he fail, he would not become the living connection between the collective consciousness of the tribe and the collective unconscious of the heroes. The challenge, then, might not be simply to integrate collective issues for his personal development, but also to show publicly how the symbolic life

---

[23] H. Jonas, *The Gnostic Religion,* p. 165.

[24] The name given to the Gnostic who was called to reunite the light that has been caught in the world with God or Father of All .

[25] Jonas, *The Gnostic Religion,* p. 187.

[26] See, for example, Elkin, *Aboriginal Men,* p. 53.

is relevant to and can benefit the greater community.

Just as the Aborigine has no difficulty in sharing "big" dreams with the tribe, so the challenge for the European, as reflected in this phase, might be to show how the collective unconscious has a contribution to make toward a better understanding of the contemporary world.

Once he has successfully negotiated the *aeons,* the pneumatic is ready to enter the center of his psyche, experience the image of the godhead and receive the revelation. This is where the Gnostic sparks are reunited, the *lapis* created and Baiame lives. It is also the realm of the Apocalyptic God, who like Baiame has light or fire coming from his eyes.[27] In addition, the Christian God's throne overlooks a sea of crystal and is surrounded by a rainbow,[28] motifs strongly associated with Baiame. Finally, while Baiame has quartz coming from each shoulder, the god of the Apocalypse is made of quartz—carnelian (red) and jasper (smoky white).[29] Thus this Christian God also embodies the opposite colors of the alchemists (red and white), representing the *lapis* or Mercurius. At this point the four traditions—Aborigine, Gnosticism, Christianity and alchemy—come together.

In view of this, the God of the Apocalypse, the Gnostic Father of All, Mercurius and Baiame all represent gods of light where the colors of the rainbow are united. It is from their realm—the unconscious—that the final revelations come.

The image of the postulant entering the world of Baiame is similar to that of Mercurius finally being raised from earth and transformed into spirit.[30] The transformation of the postulant from matter into spirit is reinforced by the fact that he receives feathered wings as part of the process of receiving Baiame's revelation. The figures of the medicine-man and Mercurius, and particularly Mercurius duplex, are virtually the same. It is Mercurius duplex who has a double nature;

---

[27] Revelation to John 1:4, Revised Standard Version.

[28] Ibid., 4:3-6.

[29] Ibid., 4:3.

[30] "The Spirit Mercurius," *Alchemical Studies,* par. 279.

he can "descend into the earth and ascend into the heavens," as well as being "dark and light" by virtue of coming from both earth and heaven.[31] The medicine-man too, having received Baiame's revelation, has the ability to live equally comfortably in these two realms. Hence the medicine-man and Mercurius contain the double nature of body and spirit, symbolized by them being both winged and wingless; the winged state refers to the air and spirit, and the wingless to the earth and body.[32] For Paracelsus this would be the coming together of the natural and aerial natures in one body, where the lights of revelation and nature are reunited with God.

The association of the integration of opposite worlds with the growing of wings is a notion that also appears in the attainment of tao: "By means of feathers he was transformed and ascended as an immortal."[33] This parallel is especially appropriate because one of the powers that Baiame bestows on the medicine-man is an ability to create rain, linking him with the myth of the rainmaker who was able to create rain only by isolating himself from the collective and finding a right balance—achieving tao—within himself.[34]

**Hearing the Call**

Of the religious traditions mentioned so far, none can proceed without divine inspiration. The alchemist, for example, feels that his work succeeds, when it does, by the grace of God *(Deo concedente)* and is guided by both dreams and other sources of inspiration from the unconscious. The medicine-man's openness to inner voices is part of a similar process: he meets the Daramulums underground, is guided by Baiame via his father's dream and ultimately receives the secrets of his profession through Baiame's revelation.

In the Gnostic tradition the impulse to embark on the road to trans-

---

[31] Ibid.

[32] See Marie-Louise von Franz, *Alchemy: An Introduction to the Symbolism and the Psychology,* pp. 128-132.

[33] B. Laufer, *The Prehistory of Aviation,* p. 16.

[34] *Mysterium Coniunctionis,* CW 14, par. 604n.

formation must be inspired by the "Call," which can only be received by the solitary individual. The one who hears it becomes the pneumatic of the community while others are doomed to a life of *ignosia* or unconsciousness. The bearer of the Call is a messenger of the Alien God who has penetrated the *aeons* which, as we have already suggested, represent the attitudes and interests that would keep the individual unconscious. Success in overcoming the archons means that the spark can be awakened and the revelatory message delivered to the individual.

The notion of the Call has parallels in general experience, manifesting through messages in dreams, hypnagogic states and active imagination. It can also be "heard" through synchronistic events and even body reactions. At a simpler level, it can be felt as restlessness, personal disquiet, a feeling that all is not right.

The medicine-man's Call manifests initially in special psychic qualities and later in the unique ability to see ghosts. This would represent an experience in which one begins to realize there is a spiritual dimension to life, as opposed to the conventional material view. In other words, one perceives an aspect of oneself that has previously been split off from consciousness.

The notion of the Call also appears in the Christian tradition through the idea of listening to the voice of the spirit: "He who has an ear, let him hear what the Spirit says to the churches. To him who conquers I will give some of the hidden manna, and I will give him a white stone, with a new name written on the stone."[35] In Revelation, there are seven churches, seven stages in the transformation of the individual, before reaching the vault of heaven; later on, the same words are repeated, the door to heaven is opened and "he who has an ear" is allowed to enter.[36] There is also a strong alchemical image here in the form of the white stone which is the *lapis,* analogous to the quartz that the medicine-man recovers from his body. Through the white stone the individual is given a new name, symbolic of a

---

[35] Revelation 2:17.
[36] Ibid., 3:23.

soul that has been reborn in the eyes of God. Thus the postulant is given a new identity and incorporates a psychic system that includes the spirit, the world of the archetypes.

Whether such messages from the unconscious are perceived as signs from the Alien God that the individual must pursue would depend on whether the inner spark has been aroused. This in turn depends on the degree of "sleepiness" or personal unconsciousness surrounding the spark.[37]

In Gnosticism one of the impediments to the Call was the degree of "noise" that had to be overcome. For modern individuals, this appears in a preoccupation with collective values and the distractions of a busy life. More particularly it can be associated with the extraverted movement of energy characteristic of the first half of life. As Socrates observed, "When overwhelmed by tumult of passions and distractions of their wants, they cannot listen or attend to the message."[38] These images apply equally well to the aboriginal postulant, whose fate demands that he adopt an introverted, or at least introspective, attitude.

In the Gnostic tradition there is neither one voice nor one messenger. The Call reveals itself only to the individual, the nature of its revelation varying from person to person. Similarly the solitary medicine-man receives Baiame's personal revelation. In this way he becomes the link between the collective consciousness of the tribe and the collective unconscious as represented by Baiame, his representative on earth. He becomes a messenger and an Alien Man.

This process symbolizes the successful transformation of one who previously supported, and identified with, the collective, to an individual who acknowledges a center in the psyche, the Self, to which the ego is subordinate. One's relationship to this new center benefits both the individual and the collective, because without this personal link to the Self, its image would sink back into the unconscious. Knowledge of the gods would be lost; God would be dead.

---

[37] Jonas, *The Gnostic Religion,* pp. 68-73.
[38] Plutarch, *Moralia,* vol. 7, p. 451.

The consequences of failing to follow up on the experience of receiving the Call and actively pursuing what might be required of one is shown in the inspired Australian novel, *Poor Fellow My Country.* Written by a contemporary white myth maker, Xavier Herbert, the story loosely follows the Wawilak myth.

In general, it is about white and black attitudes to the land. It convincingly describes the unconscious disregard of whites for both the land and its native people, contrasting this to the ease with which Aborigines relate to their environment. The author, in the person of Jeremy, the protagonist, has a vision of the day when the two might come together to form a Creole Nation[39]—a marriage of black and white. He believes that a loving attitude toward the land is a key to the cure of the split in the country.

> The true salvation of man's souls . . . can come only through [an] all-abiding love for the wondrous thing he owes his origin to . . . Mother Earth.[40]

Jeremy and his companion, Billy, are rewarded for having such an attitude when they each meet an aboriginal messenger. They talk about their experiences in the following passage. Jeremy speaks:

> He was tall . . . taller than any man I've ever seen . . . and blacker. He was standing with arms folded, looking down at me. I could see the glint in his eyes. His skin shone like polished boot-leather in the moonlight. I wasn't scared . . . only startled . . . just as when someone you know comes on you suddenly. I was even going to ask who he was. I just opened my mouth to do so . . . when he . . . well, he just wasn't there . . . only the empty sky. But so convinced was I that it was real, that I got up and looked for tracks. Nothing, of course. An apparition.[41]

Then Billy relates a similar experience:

> I find meself awake lookin' at this big blackfella watchin' me. Real as real. Only thing is I *did* speak to him. I asked him, "Who're

---

[39] *Poor Fellow My Country,* p. 32.

[40] Ibid., p. 1296.

[41] Ibid., p. 1097.

you?" Then he vanished. I was so certain it was someone, that I roused Ninyarra, who says right off it's a *Lamala* . . . what the mob over your way call *Yalmaru* . . . a man's second Shade . . . *my Lamala.* I want him to look for tracks. He won't look. He explained to me how your *Lamala* or *Yalmaru* doesn't live in your body, like your ordinary shade, the one you're born from, your soul . . . but a familiar spirit that attaches itself to you through all your lives, to look out for you, warn you of danger, tell you what to do in trouble. Not so silly when you think about subconscious and unconscious and all that sort of modern stuff, which's only dealing with ancient things. The only thing was . . . How come I a whitefeller, to get a *Lamala?* That's what I asks Ninyarra. He says, "Now properly you belong country. That *Lamala* belong to some old blackfeller before, finish now for good. He lonely. He grab 'old of you. Now you all-same blackfeller . . . belong country!"

Jeremy drew a long shuddering breath, breathed it out, repeating the words, "Belong country!" He looked half around, into the distance, murmuring, "That's what struck me . . . if I see things like a blackfellow, then I must belong like one."

"Yeah . . . that's it . . . belongin'. I used to feel ashamed o' belongin' . . . even with halfcaste kids. Livin' in a blackman's country, with blackmen . . . like a parasite. After that experience I felt completely different."

"I do, too . . . sort of at peace with it." Jeremy reached and took up a handful of dust, let it fall sparkling in the moonlight, through his fingers. Then he asked. "Tell me . . . did you ever see your . . . your *Yalmaru* again?"

"Not like that. But I sort o' know he's round all the time. Sometimes I nearly catch sight of him . . . sort o' vanishin'. He speaks to me, too . . . in my mind. It was him told me to look out for young Prindy."

Staring, Jeremy murmured, "How wonderful!"

"You know Shakespeare, Jerry . . . 'Amlet? 'There are more things in 'Eaven and Hearth, 'Oratio, than dreamt of in your philosophy.' "

Jeremy shot out his hand. Billy gripped it.

"Countryman!" whispered Jeremy.

Billy Brew breathed it back, "Countryman!"[42]

---

[42] Ibid., pp. 1097-1098.

In aboriginal mythology, Lamala/Yalmaru represents the same phenomenon as Daramulum, both being the sons of the supreme god and his spirits and messengers. With both men having a great love for the land, they can be said to have integrated an aspect of the Great Mother. Having stirred their Eros, she introduces them to the spirit of the land, who appears in a manner fully to be expected of an alien. It is also an example of how contact with a feminine presence (Mother Earth in this case) can act as a psychopomp, leading the ego to the image of the messengers who symbolize the spiritual center of the psyche.

The words with which Ninyarra, the aboriginal, describes Yalmaru are worth repeating: "A familiar spirit that attaches itself to you through all of your lives, to look out for you, warn you of danger, tell you what to do in trouble." Compare this with Apuleius' description of Socrates' genius or daemon as "a private patron and individual guide, guardian of one's own welfare . . . [who] can give warnings in a desperate situation, can protect us in dangerous situations."[43]

Socrates and Ninyarra are describing the same thing, a personal experience of the Self, in almost identical language. Ninyarra voices the same words that were uttered on another continent separated by distance and millennia. Time and place come together here. The result is a statement which yields the secret of the psychological source of the messenger, the collective unconscious.

After Jeremy has had this experience his life falls apart and there is a sad and destructive ending. The heroine is drowned and Jeremy dies as well. Another positive figure, Jonkers, becomes an expatriot and emigrates because he feels he can no longer live in a country so split between black and white. Prindy, the young Aborigine caught between his own world and Jeremy's, is killed.

Prindy is the young man sought throughout the story by a medicine-man to enter an age-grading ceremony and possibly suc-

---

[43] From a translation of Apuleius, "Deo Socratis," quoted by Marie-Louise von Franz in *Projection and Re-Collection in Jungian Psychology*, p. 149.

ceed him as the medicine-man. However, while Prindy is undergoing an initiatory trial, Jeremy interrupts out of fear that it could be dangerous. Ironically, his impulsive action and unexpected arrival result in the accidental death of young Prindy, and so he is killed not by the black men but indirectly by the white protagonist.

Taken symbolically, Jeremy was driven to prevent his own young aboriginal spirit from being initiated. As a result he killed off any chance that this figure could become his inner medicine-man who would link him not only with the unconscious, but also with the instinctive and archetypal nature of the land. This would be equivalent to Yurlunggur integrating Lumaluma. By responding to the situation with his one-sided white morality, Jeremy effectively became his own archon and prevented the development of his native spirit. His chances of redeeming the two aspects of his personality, black and white, were therefore doomed. When forced to act quickly his well-worn Christian morality took over and killed his aboriginal potential. Disoriented by his panic, he instinctively grasped for what he knew best. He forgot to consider Lamala as another point of orientation.

Although Jeremy had a personal experience of the spirit of the land, he did not understand or accept its meaning. In effect, he had produced the quartz from his body by experiencing the vision of Lamala-Daramulum, but failed to realize that he was encountering an essential part of himself, the spiritual side. In a similar vein his notion of a Creole Nation was biological rather than spiritual; he failed to perceive this idea as a symbolic integration of the two lights, one from the dark earth and the other from the light of heaven. He saw his vision objectively in its extraverted form and missed its symbolic value. He even looked for Lamala's tracks after he disappeared! In effect, he regarded the vision merely as a compliment that he had become part of the country; he failed to see it as a religious image around which he could address the split in the land and in himself.

Contrast his attitude with that of Billy, his personal shadow, the only hero in the novel who survives, representing the glimmer of hope that a national split can ultimately be healed through an individual's experience.

From Billy's statements it is clear that through a type of active imagination he was able to engage the spirit of his Shade in everyday life. As he states, he was able to "catch sight of him . . . speaks to me, too . . . in my mind." Thus he not only established a creative relationship with an image of the Self, he also became sensitive to the message of his inner daemon. This is what Jeremy failed to do and it resulted in his death, while Billy survived to wander the country with his black and white soul. In this sense he combined the nomadic spirit of both the black and early white myth makers because he respected the message he received and followed it along his meandering individual path. He was able to acknowledge the wisdom contained in "'Eaven and Hearth" (heaven and earth); he realized that the light of nature and the light of revelation were superior to Jeremy's educated notions concerning the meaning of life.

By being humble enough to hear the Call, Billy proved himself to be unlike Jeremy. Rather, like the medicine-man, he was able to produce the quartz from his body and recognize that he had been blessed with a special experience. He embarked on the path to individuation while Jeremy died with a split soul, having failed to develop a creative relationship with the center of the psyche, the Self. Thus Jeremy represents an unhealed personal and national split, whereas Billy is the symbol of a personality and country that is undivided.

There is no prescription for individuation, but one of the basic notions includes an ability to establish a living relationship with the unconscious. One must have the courage to listen to the message that emanates from this irrational world and then to follow its directions. We can turn to Socrates again and his experience with his daemon, to see how his approach to this inner figure was similar to Billy's and at variance with Jeremy's.

Socrates' attitude epitomizes a creative relationship with the spiritual center. In the *Moralia* we hear the cynical comments of those who regard listening to voices and acting on their direction as "humbug and superstition."[44] However we are also told that

---

[44] Plutarch, *Moralia,* vol. 7, p. 401.

Socrates constantly listened for the voice of his daemon; it was a divine being which "showed him the way, illumining his path."[45] If he recognized the sign, Socrates would act in accordance with its directions. These came not only in the form of dreams or visions, but also in a voiceless contact by which the daemon's higher intelligence was able to touch Socrates' thoughts, much as Yalmaru contacted Billy: "He speaks to me, too, . . . in my mind."

Simmias describes the nature of Socrates' daemon while at the same time keeping the mystery completely alive and unresolved:

> [Through] the perception of a voice or else the mental apprehension of language that reached him in some strange way . . . Socrates . . . had an understanding which . . . was so sensitive and delicate as to respond at once to what reached him. What reached him . . . was not spoken language, but the unuttered words of a daemon, making voiceless contact with his intelligence by their sense alone . . . the intelligence of the higher power guides the gifted soul, which requires no blows, by the touch of its thought.[46]

Such messages were thought to pass through all men but to find a receptive ear only in the daemonic or holy man.

The coincidence of the light motif and the personal experience with the Self, as well as the mysterious relationship between the two, are further summed up by Simmias:

> The thoughts of the daemons [are] luminous and shed their light on the daemonic man.[47]

Billy was the daemonic man and actively carried the light of the spirit of the land. The Rainbow Serpent spoke to him and Billy heard his voice.

---

[45] Ibid., p. 405 (from Homer, *Iliad,* xx, 95; cf. *Odyssey,* xix, 34).

[46] Ibid., pp. 451-453.

[47] Ibid., p. 455.

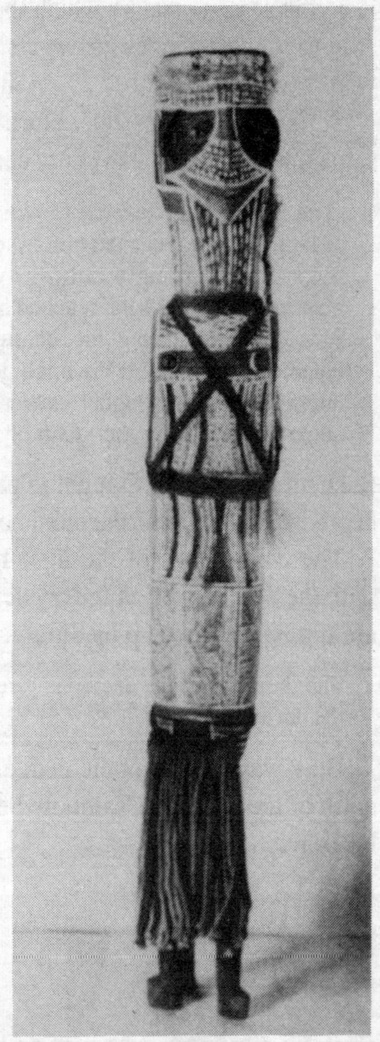

*Left: Djuwei* post representing the elder Wawilak sister.
*Right:* Wooden image of the younger Wawilak sister.
(From R.M. Berndt, "Australian Aboriginal Religion")

# Appendix
## Myth of the Wawilak Women[*]

### A. The Coming of the Two Sisters from the Southern Interior

*1. The two sisters and their children leave the Wawilak country and start toward the sea, naming the animals and plants as they go; but before they leave they have incestuous relations with their clansmen from which a child is born later in the Wawilak country.*

It was the time of Bamun (the mythological period) when Wongar men walked about and modern man had not yet appeared. Everything was different. Animals were like men then! Those two Wawilak sisters had come a long distance. They were coming from the far interior to the Arafura Sea. They had come from the far interior Kardao Kardao country. This is a clan territory of the Dua moiety. They had come from the land of the Wawilak people for Kardao Kardao is their country. The wirkul (a young woman who has not had a child) was pregnant. The gungmun (a woman who has had a child: literally, "the giver") carried her own baby under her arm in a paper-bark "cradle." It was a male child.

The two women carried stone spears and hawks' down and bush cotton. On the way they killed iguana, opossum, and bandicoot for their food. They also gathered some bush yams (ippa). When they killed the animals, they gave them the names they bear today; they did the same for the yam. They gathered all the plants and animals that are in the Murngin country today. They said to each thing they killed or gathered, "You will be maraiin [a totemic emblem] by and by."

When the two sisters started their journey they talked Djaun, later Rainbarngo, and still later Djinba; then they talked Wawilak, and finally Liaalaomir. They named the country as they went along. In the Wawilak country they copulated with Wawilak Wongar men. These men were Dua, and they were Dua. This was very wrong and asocial.

The two women stopped to rest, for the younger felt the child she was carrying move inside her. She knew her baby would soon be born.

"Yeppa [sister], I feel near my heart this baby turning," she said.

The older one said, "Then let us rest."

---

[*] From W. Lloyd Warner, *A Black Civilization: A Social Study of an Australian Tribe.*

They sat down, and the older sister put her hand on the abdomen of the younger sister and felt the child moving inside. She then massaged her younger sister, for she knew the labour pains had commenced. The baby was born there. It was Yiritja, for its mother was Dua. The country was still a part of the territory of the Wawilak clan.

After the child was born the older sister gathered more bush food, then the two moved on toward the sea. They stopped at various places and gave all of them names. They named all the clan territories and the localities within their borders. They first rested at Djirri Djirri (quail place), then at Wakngay (crow place), Dung Dunga (fish spear place), Tarbella (white oyster place), and Katatanga (falling meteor place). All these localities were Dua and were within the country of the Wawilak clan. Although the Wawilak sisters went to almost all the clans of the Dua moeity they never walked on the country of the Yiritja moeity.

"Come on, sister," said the older, "we'll go quickly now." They drank water at the last place and hurried on.

## 2. The flight of the food animals

They did not stop until they sat down at the great Mirrirmina (rock python's back) water hole in the country of the Liaalaomir clan. It is in the bottom of this well in the deep subterranean waters below the upper waters that Yurlunggur, the great copper snake, or python totem of the Dua moeity, lives. They called the country for the first time Mirrirmina.

The older sister took her fire drill and made a fire. She started cooking all the yams and other bush food that she had gathered and all the animals that they had killed on their journey.

"Sister, you cook my food for me, too," said the younger one.

"Be patient," said the older. She then gathered some paper bark and fashioned a bed for her younger sister's newborn child. As she did this, she said, "By and by, sister, we must circumcise these two small sons of ours."

"Yes, sister," said the younger.

As soon as they cooked the food each animal and plant jumped out of the fire and ran to the Mirrirmina water hole and jumped into it. They all went into this Djungguan and Gunabibi well. The crab ran in first. When he did this, the two women talked Liaalaomir for the first time; before this they had talked Wawilak. The other plants and animals followed the crab. The yams ran like men, as did the iguanas, frill-neck lizard, darpa, ovarku snake, rock python, sea gull, sea eagles, native companion and crocodiles. Each ran and dived into the clans' totemic well and disappeared from sight.

## B. The Python's Sacred Pool Is Profaned and He Swallows the Wawilak Women

### 3. The profanement of the pool

The older woman went out to gather bark to make a bed for her sister's baby after it was born. She walked over some of the water of the Mirrirmina well. Her menstrual blood fell in the totem well and was carried down the sacred water hole, where Yurlunggur, the Big Father, lives.

### 4. Yurlunggur raises himself to swallow the women; the rain comes and the flood commences covering the earth.

When menstrual blood dropped into the pool Yurlunggur smelled the odor of this pollution from where he was lying in the black water beneath the floor of the totem well. His head was lying quietly on the bottom of the pit. He raised his head and smelled again and again.

"Where does this blood come from?" he said. He opened the bottom of the well by throwing the stone which covers its base out of the well on to the land by the women's camp. (The stone is near the camp today and can be seen by those who go there. "It's now a snake's head.") He crawled out slowly, like a snake does, from the well. When he came out he sucked some of the well water into his mouth. He spat it into the sky. Soon a cloud about the size of a man's hand appeared from nowhere in the center of the sky. As Yurlunggur slowly rose from out of the bottom of the pool the totemic well water rose too and flooded the earth. He pulled himself up on the stone which he had thrown, and laid his head there. He looked around him. He saw the women and their babies. Yurlunggur was older brother to these women, and they were sisters to him. Their children were his wakus, and he was gawel to them.

Yurlunggur continued to look at them. He hissed. This was to call out for rain. There was no cloud in the sky until then, but soon the two sisters saw a small, a very small, black cloud appear in the heavens. They did not see the great python lying there watching them.

The cloud grew larger and larger, and soon the rain came down. The Wawilak sisters hurriedly built a house to be ready for the rain. They named the forked sticks they used as uprights. The women went inside the house. They did not know where this rain came from; they did not know that the older sister's menstrual blood had defiled the Mirrirmina water hole and had made Yurlunggur angry.

The Wawilak women went to sleep, but the rain poured down harder and harder and awakened them.

### *5. The sisters sing the rituals to prevent the flood and the snake swallowing them.*

The gungmun said, "Sister, where does this rain come from? There's no cloud in the north or south, and there is no cloud in the east or west, but over us is this huge black cloud. I think something is wrong. I think something terrible is going to happen."

She got up and went outside. The younger one stayed within the house and sang. The gungmun beat the ground with her yam stick; she knew now that Yurlunggur was going to swallow her, and she wanted to stop the rain. She sang, "Yurlunggur, don't you come out and swallow us. We are good, and we are clean." While she sang she danced around the house. the two sisters then called out the taboo names of the Mirrirmina well.

While the older sister sang and danced around the house, and the younger sister sang inside it to stop the rain coming down and to drive the great cloud away, they were being surrounded by all the snakes in the land. The pythons, death adders, tree snakes, black snakes, tiger snakes, iguanas, the blue-tongued lizard, snails, caterpillars, and all the Dua snakes came up around them in a circle, for they had heard the call of their father, Yurlunggur. It was night and the women did not see them.

The gungmun first sang all the songs sung in the general camp during Gunabibi. These are the less powerful songs. She did this first, for she thought they would stop the rain, but it did not stop. She was afraid of this rain, for it came out of a cloud she could not understand, because this cloud had come from nowhere.

She sang then the taboo songs of the Djungguan—"Ah! Ah! Ah! Kak Ye!!!" She sang the songs when the subsection names are called out in Djungguan. She took the Dua subsections first.

The young sister sang like the leader of the Djungguan ceremony does today. She kept time with singing sticks. She said, "We'll turn to the Yiritja subsections now. We'll call out the Yiritja peoples [subsections]."

They sang the garma songs first, for they are not "strong" and belong to the camp of the women. Then they sang the songs of the Marndiella, for it is only a little more powerful, and its songs only slightly more taboo. Then they sang Djungguan and Ulmark.

The rain continued and came down harder and harder. They decided that they must sing something even more powerful, more taboo, and deeper within the ceremonial camp of the men.

### *6. Yurlunggur swallows the women, and the earth is covered with a flood.*

They sang Yurlunggur and menstrual blood.

When Yurlunggur heard these words, he crawled into the camp of the two women and their two children. They had suddenly fallen into a deep sleep from his magic. He licked the women and children all over preparatory to swallowing them. He bit the noses of each and made the blood come. He swallowed the old woman first, the wirkul next, and the little boys last.

He waited for daylight. When dawn came he uncoiled and went out a short distance in the bush, because he was too near the water. He wanted to leave the women in a dry place.

He raised himself and stood very straight. He was like the trunk of a very tall straight tree. His head reached as high as a cloud. When he raised himself to the sky the flood waters came up as he did. They flooded and covered the entire earth. No tree or hill showed above them. When he fell later, the water receded, and at the same time there was dry ground. While he was high in the sky and had the two women and children inside him he sang all the Marndiella, Djungguan, Gunabibi and Ulmark ceremonies.

7. *The Dua clan snakes and Yurlunggur discuss what they have eaten and discover that they have different languages but the same totemic emblems. They tell their language names, the names of their totemic water holes, and recite the list of their totems, and kinship is established.*

The other Wongar Wirtits (totemic pythons) stood up too. They were all Dua, as Yurlunggur was, and none was Yiritja. Yurlunggur was higher than all the rest. He was the leader for those other snakes, and was more powerful than they.

The Wessel Island python (Perango clan) raised himself. "What is your language?" he said.

"I am Liaalaomir. What is yours?"

"I am Perango Yaernungo."

"What is yours?" Yurlunggur then said to the python on the Howard Island mainland.

"I am Liagaomir."

"What is yours?" he asked the Banyan Island python.

"I am Karmalanga language. My country is Kolpaiyunala."

The Mandelpui, Wawilak, Boun, Djirin, Kalpu, Merango, Djapu, Djawark, and all Dua clans were asked by Yurlunggur what their language was, and each answered the language of his country.

The Mirrirmina snake said then, "I see we all talk different languages. It would be better if we talked the same tongue. We can't help this now. It is better then that we all have our ceremonies together, for we own the same maraiin."

They all sang out together then, and their voices were thunder and roared all over the land and sea.

The python Wongars still stood on their tails high in the sky. The great Yurlunggur turned to a Daii Dua snake. He said, "What have you been eating?"

"I have been eating fresh-water fish" (Dua variety).

"How did he taste?"

"Oh, he was very good. Nice and fat."

"What are you going to do, now that you have eaten him?"

"I'm going to spew him up and look at him and eat him again for the last time."

He was going to do what the live pythons do now; they eat something, swallow it, spew it up, lick it, and eat it again. It does not come up again.

Yurlunggur now asked the Djapu python what he had eaten.

"I ate wallaby [Dua moeity]. I'm going to let him out."

He inquired of the others. The Merango snake had eaten a small plains bird; the Kalpu, a sand crab; Djirin, a green sea turtle; Naladaer, a small shellfish; Wawilak, a bird; Mandelpui, a fresh- water fish; Karmalanga, honey. All the snakes of the Dua clan were asked. Wessel Island snake was asked last. He is second highest and only lower in rank than Mirrirmina.

"What have you been eating?" the Liaalaomir snake asked the Wessel Island one.

"I won't tell you."

"Come on, you and I are brothers. Remember I call you brother."

"If I tell you, you must tell me, because I call you wawa [older brother] and you called me yukiyuko [younger brother] just as you said."

"I'll tell you. I've eaten parrot fish."

"What colour?"

"Blue."

"What kind of teeth?"

"White."

"What you have eaten is no good. Why didn't you eat iguana or stone kangaroo?"

"But what did you eat?" replied the Wessel Island snake.

"I won't tell you."

"Why not?"

The Mirrirmina snake raised itself higher and higher into the sky. He laid his neck and head on a cloud. His eyes shot lightning. He felt ashamed.

"Come on and tell me, my big brother," said the Wessel Island snake again.

The Wessel Island snake continued to insist, and his head came closer as his body writhed across the clouds toward the Mirrirmina python. He was very angry.

After a long time Yurlunggur said, "I ate two sisters and a small boy and girl."

8. *The fall of Yurlunggur and the decline of the flood when the southeastern wind blows.*

When he said this the southeastern monsoon started blowing from off the land. As it did the head of the Wessel Island snake hurriedly pulled back to its own well. The wind had stopped him from coming farther; he wanted to make a waterway from Wessel Island to Mirrirmina. Yurlunggur roared and fell to the ground the same time.

When he fell, he split the ground open and made the present dance ground at the Liaalaomir ceremonial place. He lay there on the ground and thought, "Those two sisters and their children are dead inside me now."

Yurlunggur started cleansing his mouth with his cheeks and tongue. He spat several times. He said to his sons, "I'm going to spew." He regurgitated the two women and the little boys. They were dropped into an ants' nest.

The Wessel Island snake, when he heard what Yurlunggur said, was disgusted. "You've eaten your own wakus and yeppas," he said. This was a terrible thing.

9. *The totemic trumpet appears and Yurlunggur goes back to the Mirrirmina water hole where he gathers all the snake creatures, returns, and reswallows the women and once again falls and the flood is ended.*

The Wongar Yurlunggur crawled slowly back to his water hole. He went inside but kept his head up to watch. At this time the Yurlunggur trumpet came out of the well and lay beside him. No one brought it out and no one blew it, but it sang out like it does now.

The Yurlunggur trumpet blew over the two women and their two sons. They were lying there like they had fainted. Some green ants came out then and bit the women and children. They jumped.

The trumpet continued to walk around, while the Wongar Yurlunggur looked on. The women and children were alive again, and he had thought them dead. He picked up two singing sticks (bilmel) and crawled out of the water hole. Before he emerged he called all his sons, who were in the well, and put these true snakes, lizards, and snails on his head and neck.

He hit the mothers and their babies on their heads with the sticks and swallowed them again. He meant to keep them down this time.

He felt sick again, for once more he had swallowed Dua people. He decided to stand up straight.

When he raised up the mandelpui snake shouted, "What did you eat?"

"Bandicoot," he lied.

"You do not tell the truth."

"The two Dua women and the two Yiritja boys."

When he said this he fell again. This time he made the Gunabibi and Ulmark dance grounds by his fall (as the first time he fell he formed a Djungguan place). After his fall, he crawled into the Liaalaomir well and went down into the subterranean waters. He put a stone over his entrance and stopped the flood of water that had been coming out. He swam in the underground waters to the Wawilak country, for he wanted to take the mothers and children back to their own country; here he spat them out for the last time. He left them there and came back to his own country. The two women turned to stone and one can still see them in the Wawilak country today. Yurlunggur kept the boys inside him, for they were Yiritja and he was Dua.

The two women did not circumcise their two sons as they intended, because Yurlunggur had interfered before they were ready. It was because they so intended, and said for other people to perform this act, that people cut their sons today.

## C. Man Learns the Secrets of the Creator Sisters' Rituals

*10. Man learns the secrets of the Wawilak women and at this time starts the use of these rituals by modern men through using women's blood and the ritual paraphernalia brought with them to Mirrirmina. Man is warned by the women in a dream to continue to practice these ceremonies forever.*

While all this great drama was being acted in the country of the Liaalaomir, the two Wawilak Wongar men had heard the terrible noise of the snake's voice (thunder) and they had seen the skies fill with lightning and felt the downpour of the rain. They knew something was the matter, so they followed the two women's tracks. It took them many days and nights to get there. They finally saw the snake track.

"I think the sisters had trouble," said one. "I think that maybe a crocodile or python has killed them."

They arrived at Mirrirmina. They had followed the Goyder River down. They saw all the ants walking around everywhere, like they smelled something that was dead and they wanted to eat. They then found all the snake tracks. The well water shone like a rainbow. When they saw this they knew there was a snake in there.

They went farther in the bush and saw the ceremonial ground where Yurlunggur's fall had made the dance places.

"Wongar python has been here," they said.

When they looked carefully at the stone, they found blood from the heads of the two women and boys.

"What will we do?"

"Run and get some paper bark and make a basket," said the older Wawilak man.

They gathered two baskets of blood, and went to the dance grounds. They made a bush house on part of the ground that represents the snake's tail.

"You take all the hawk's feathers, bush cotton, and this blood, and we'll paint ourselves. You do this, and I shall go cut a hollow log and make a Yurlunggur trumpet."

Each did his task. The hollow ridgepole from the Wawilak sisters' house was used for the trumpet totemic emblem of Yurlunggur.

The sun went down. They left the blood till morning. They slept, and while they were in a deep sleep they dreamed of what the two women sang and danced when they were trying to keep Yurlunggur from swallowing them. The Wawilak women came back as spirits and taught the two men the Djungguan songs and dances that are for the outside general camp, and the inside ones that are for the men's camp. They told the men the way to do the Marndiella, Gunabibi and Ulmark ceremonies. They sang Yurlunggur and Muit. The men slept on and dreamed that Yurlunggur brought out all the iguanas from the Mirrirmina well.

The two sisters said to men, "This is all now. We are giving you this dream so you can remember these important things. You must never forget these things we have told you tonight. You must remember every time each year these songs and dances. You must paint with blood and feathers for the Marndiella, Gunabibi and Djungguan. You must dance all the things we saw and named on our journey, and which ran away into the well."

After the men danced the new dances and ceremonies for the first time they went back to their own country. "We dance these things now, because our Wongar ancestors learned them from the two Wawilak sisters."

# Bibliography


*Australian Year Book, 1987.* Canberra: HMSO, 1988.

Barker, E., ed. and trans. *The Politics of Aristotle.* London: Oxford University Press, 1958.

Baynes, H.G. *Mythology of the Soul.* London: Methuen & Co., 1949.

Berndt, R. M. "Australian Aboriginal Religion." *Iconography of Religions*, vols. 1 and 2. Institute of Religious Iconography. Leiden: E.J. Brill, 1974.

__________. *Djanggawul.* London: Routledge & Kegan Paul, 1952.

__________. "Images of God in Aboriginal Australia." *Visible Religion,* vol. 2. Leiden: E.J. Brill, 1985.

__________. *Kunapipi: A Study of an Australian Aboriginal Cult.* Melbourne: F.W. Cheshire, 1951.

__________. "Wuradjeri Magic and Clever Men." *Oceania,* vol. 17, no. 4 (1946-47).

Berndt, R.M. and Berndt, C.H. *The World of the First Australians.* Sydney: Ure Smith, 1976.

Brodie, A. *Kunwinjku Bim.* Melbourne: National Gallery, 1984.

Buchler, I.R. and Maddock, K. *The Rainbow Serpent: A Chromatic Piece.* The World Anthology Series. The Hague: Mouton, 1978.

Campbell, J. *The Mythic Image.* (Bollingen Series C). Princeton: Princeton University Press, 1974.

Edinger, E. *Anatomy of the Psyche: Alchemical Symbolism in Psychotherapy.* La Salle, IL: Open Court, 1985.

Elkin, A.P. *Aboriginal Men of High Degree.* St. Lucia: University of Queensland Press, 1977.

__________. "The Rainbow Serpent Myth in North-West Australia." *Oceania,* vol. 1, no. 3 (1930).

Eliade, M. *Australian Religions.* Ithaca: Cornell University Press, 1973.

__________. *The Forge and the Crucible.* 2nd. ed. Chicago: Chicago University Press, 1978.

__________. *From Primitives To Zen.* New York: Harper & Row, 1977.

__________. *Patterns In Comparative Religion.* New York: Sheed & Ward, 1952.

________. *Rites and Symbols of Initiation.* New York: Harper Torchbooks, 1975.

________. *Shamanism.* New York: Pantheon, 1965.

Freud, Sigmund. *Totem and Taboo.* New York: Vintage Books, 1918.

Furst, Peter T. "The Shamanic Universe." In *Stones, Bones, and Skin: Ritual and Shamanic Art.* Toronto: Arts Canada, 1973.

*Gospel According to Thomas.* New York: Concord Grove Press, 1983.

Grimm Brothers. *The Complete Grimm's Fairy Tales.* New York: Pantheon Books, 1944.

Harding, M.Esther. *Woman's Mysteries, Ancient and Modern.* New York: Harper Colophon, 1971.

Herbert, X. *Poor Fellow My Country.* Sydney: William Collins, 1977.

Hiatt, L.R., ed. *Australian Aboriginal Mythology.* Australian Institute of Aboriginal Studies. Carlton, NSW: Excelsis Press, 1975.

Howitt, A.W. *The Native Tribes of South-East Australia.* London: Macmillan, 1904.

Hughes, R. *The Fatal Shore.* London: Pan Books, 1988.

Huxley, Francis. *The Way of the Sacred.* New York: Doubleday, 1974.

Isaacs, J. *Australian Aboriginal Paintings.* Willoughby, NSW: Weldon Publishing, 1989.

Jonas, H. *The Gnostic Religion.* Boston: Beacon Hill, 1963.

Jung, C.G. *The Collected Works of C.G. Jung* (Bollingen Series XX), 20 vols. Trans. R.F.C. Hull. Ed. H. Read, M. Fordham, G. Adler, Wm. McGuire. Princeton: Princeton University Press, 1953-1979.

________. *Alchemy: Notes on Lectures Given at the Eidgenössische Technische Hochschule, Zurich, 1940-1941.* Privately printed.

________. "Approaching the Unconscious." In *Man and His Symbols,* ed. C.G. Jung. London: Aldus Books, 1964.

________. *C.G. Jung Letters.* 2 vols. Ed. G. Adler and A. Jaffé. London: Routledge & Kegan Paul, 1973 & 1976.

________. *Dream Analysis: Notes of the Seminar Given in 1928-1930* (Bollingen Series XCIX). Ed. Wm. McGuire. Princeton: Princeton University Press, 1984.

________. *Memories, Dreams, Reflections.* Ed. Aniela Jaffé. New York: Vintage, 1965.

________. *The Visions Seminars.* 2 vols. Zürich: Spring, 1976.

Jung, Emma and von Franz, Marie-Louise. *The Grail Legend.* 2nd ed. Boston: Sigo Press, 1986.

Kerényi, C. *The Gods Of The Greeks.* London: Thames & Hudson, 1951.

Lawson, H. *Winnowed Verses.* Sydney: Angus & Robertson, 1944.

Laufer, B. *The Prehistory of Aviation.* The Anthropological Series, vol. 18, no. 1. Chicago: Field Museum of Natural History, 1928.

Layard, J. "Identification With The Sacrificial Animal." *Eranos Jahrbuch,* vol. 24 (1955).

________. "The Making of Man in Malekula." *Eranos Jahrbuch,* vol. 16 (1948).

________. *The Virgin Archetype.* New York: Spring Publications, 1972.

Lévy-Strauss, C. *The Savage Mind.* London: Weidenfeld & Nicholson, 1966.

Loewenstein, J. "Rainbow and Serpent." *Anthropos,* vol. 56 (1961).

McConnel, U. "The Rainbow Serpent In North Queensland." *Oceania,* vol. 1, no. 3 (1930).

Meggit, M.J. "Gadjari: Among the Walbiri Aborigines of Central Australia," *Oceania Monograph no. 14.* Sydney: University of Sydney, 1967.

Montagu, A. *Coming into Being Among the Australian Aborigines.* London: Routledge & Kegan Paul, 1974.

Pagels, E. *The Gnostic Gospels.* New York: Vintage Books, 1981.

Palmer, V. *The Legend of the Nineties.* Melbourne: Melbourne University Press, 1954.

Piddington, R. "The Water-Serpent in Karadjeri Mythology." *Oceania,* vol. 1, no. 3 (1930).

Plutarch. *Moralia,* vol. 7. Cambridge: Cambridge University Press, 1959.

Quispel, G. "Gnosis and the New Sayings of Jesus." *Eranos Jahrbuch,* 1969.

Roderick, C., ed. *Henry Lawson: Autobiographical and Other Writings, 1887-1922.* 2 vols. Sydney: Angus & Robertson, 1972.

________. *Henry Lawson: Criticism.* Sydney: Angus & Robertson, 1972.

________. *Henry Lawson: Short Stories and Sketches,* vol. 1. Sydney: Angus & Robertson, 1972.

Radcliffe-Brown, A.R. "The Rainbow Serpent in South-East Australia." *Oceania,* vol. 1, no. 3 (1930).

Róheim, G. *The Eternal Ones of the Dream: A Psychoanalytic Interpretation of Australian Myth and Ritual.* New York: International Universities Press, 1945.

Rudolph, K. *Gnosis.* New York: Harper & Row, 1983.

Spencer, B. *The Native Tribes of the Northern Territory.* London: Macmillan, 1914.

Spencer, B. and Gillen, F.J. *The Native Tribes of Central Australia.* London: Macmillan, 1899.

Stanner, W.E.H. *Australian Aboriginal Studies.* London: Oxford University Press, 1964.

Sutton, P., ed. *Dreamings: The Art of Aboriginal Australia.* Ringwood, Vic.: Viking, 1988.

Turner, V. *The Ritual Process.* Ithaca: Cornell University Press, 1977.

von Franz, Marie-Louise. *Alchemy: An Introduction to the Symbolism and the Psychology.* Toronto: Inner City Books, 1980.

__________. *C.G. Jung: His Myth in Our Time.* New York: G.P. Putnam's Sons, for the C.G. Jung Foundation for Analytical Psychology, 1975.

__________. *On Dreams And Death.* Boston: Shambhala, 1976.

__________. *Projection and Re-Collection in Jungian Psychology.* La Salle, IL: Open Court, 1981.

__________. *Puer Aeternus: A Psychological Study of the Adult Struggle with the Paradise of Childhood.* Santa Monica: Sigo Press, 1981.

__________. *Redemption Motifs in Fairytales.* Toronto: Inner City Books, 1980.

Wallace-Crabbe, C. "Lawson's Joe Wilson." *Australian Literary Studies,* vol. 1, no. 3 (1964).

Ward, R. *Australia Since the Coming of Man.* New York: Lansdowne Press, 1982.

Warner, W.Lloyd. *A Black Civilization: A Social Study of an Australian Tribe.* New York: Harper Torchbooks, 1958.

White, V. "Some Notes on Gnosticism." *Spring 1949.*

Wilhelm, R., trans. *The I Ching or Book of Changes* (Bollingen Series XIX). Princeton: Princeton University Press, 1971.

# Index